Ce

D0918626

THE STORY OF A CANNONEER UNDER STONEWALL JACKSON

GENERAL "STONEWALL" JACKSON

The Story of a Cannoneer
Under Stonewall Jackson

IN WHICH IS TOLD THE PART TAKEN BY THE
ROCKBRIDGE ARTILLERY IN THE ARMY
OF NORTHERN VIRGINIA

BY

EDWARD A. MOORE

WITH INTRODUCTIONS BY

CAPT. ROBERT E. LEE, Jr., AND HON. HENRY
ST. GEORGE TUCKER

Fully Illustrated by Portraits

BOOKS FOR LIBRARIES PRESS
FREEPORT, NEW YORK

First Published 1907
Reprinted 1971

INTERNATIONAL STANDARD BOOK NUMBER:
0-8369-5633-8

LIBRARY OF CONGRESS CATALOG CARD NUMBER:
77-146866

PRINTED IN THE UNITED STATES OF AMERICA

To the Spartan Mother

WHO UNFLINCHINGLY SENT HER FOUR SONS
TO THE FIELD

AND

To the Wife

WITHOUT WHOSE ASSISTANCE AND ENCOURAGEMENT
IT WOULD NEVER HAVE BEEN WRITTEN,
THIS VOLUME IS AFFECTIONATELY
DEDICATED

PREFACE

More than thirty years ago, at the solicitation of my kinsman, H. C. McDowell, of Kentucky, I undertook to write a sketch of my war experience. McDowell was a major in the Federal Army during the civil war, and with eleven first cousins, including Gen. Irvin McDowell, fought against the same number of first cousins in the Confederate Army. Various interruptions prevented the completion of my work at that time. More recently, after despairing of the hope that some more capable member of my old command, the Rockbridge Artillery, would not allow its history to pass into oblivion, I resumed the task, and now present this volume as the only published record of that company, celebrated as it was even in that matchless body of men, the Army of Northern Virginia.

E. A. M.

CONTENTS

LIST OF ILLUSTRATIONS

INTRODUCTION BY CAPT. ROBERT E. LEE, JR.

THE title of this book at once rivets attention and invites perusal, and that perusal does not disappoint expectation. The author was a cannoneer in the historic Rockbridge (Va.) Artillery, which made for itself, from Manassas to Appomattox, a reputation second to none in the Confederate service. No more vivid picture has been presented of the private soldier in camp, on the march, or in action. It was written evidently not with any commercial view, but was an undertaking from a conviction that its performance was a question of duty to his comrades. Its unlabored and spontaneous character adds to its value. Its detail is evidence of a living presence, intent only upon truth. It is not only carefully planned, but minutely finished. The duty has been performed faithfully and entertainingly.

We are glad these delightful pages have not been marred by discussion of the causes or conduct of the great struggle between the States. There is no theorizing or special pleading to distract our attention from the unvarnished story of the Confederate soldier.

The writer is simple, impressive, and sincere. And his memory is not less faithful. It is a striking and truthful portrayal of the times under the standard of one of the greatest generals of ancient or modern times. It is from such books that data will be gathered by the future historian for a true story of the great conflict between the States.

For nearly a year (from March to November, 1862) I served in the battery with this cannoneer, and for a time we were in the same mess. Since the war I have known him intimately, and it gives me great pleasure to be able to say that there is no one who could give a more honest and truthful account of the events of our struggle from the standpoint of a private soldier. He had exceptional opportunities for observing men and events, and has taken full advantage of them.

ROBERT E. LEE.

INTRODUCTION BY HENRY ST. GEORGE TUCKER

BETWEEN 1740 and 1750 nine brothers by the name of Moore emigrated from the north of Ireland to America. Several of them settled in South Carolina, and of these quite a number participated in the Revolutionary War, several being killed in battle. One of the nine brothers, David by name, came to Virginia and settled in the "Borden Grant," now the northern part of Rockbridge County. There, in 1752, his son, afterward known as Gen. Andrew Moore, was born. His mother was a Miss Evans, of Welsh ancestry. Andrew Moore was educated at an academy afterward known as Liberty Hall. In early life with some of his companions he made a voyage to the West Indies; was shipwrecked, but rescued, after many hardships, by a passing vessel and returned to the Colonies. Upon his return home he studied law in the office of Chancellor Wythe, at Williamsburg, and was licensed to practice law in 1774. In 1776 he entered the army as lieutenant, in Morgan's Riflemen, and was engaged in those battles which resulted in the capture of Burgoyne's army, and at the surrender of the British forces at Saratoga. For courage and gallantry in battle he was promoted to a captaincy. Having served three

2

years with Morgan, he returned home and took his seat as a member of the Virginia legislature, taking such an active and distinguished part in the deliberations of that body that he was elected to Congress, and as a member of the first House of Representatives was distinguished for his services to such a degree that he was re-elected at each succeeding election until 1797, when he declined further service in that body, but accepted a seat in the Virginia House of Delegates. He was again elected to Congress in 1804, but in the first year of his service he was elected to the United States Senate, in which body he served with distinguished ability until 1809, when he retired. He was then appointed United States Marshal for the District of Virginia, which office he held until his death, April 14, 1821. His brother William served as a soldier in the Indian wars, and the Revolutionary War. He was a lieutenant of riflemen at Pt. Pleasant, and carried his captain, who had been severely wounded, from the field of battle, after killing the Indian who was about to scalp him—a feat of courage and strength rarely equaled. Gen. Andrew Moore's wife was Miss Sarah Reid, a descendant of Capt. John McDowell, who was killed by the Indians, December 18, 1742, on James River, in Rockbridge County. She was the daughter of Capt. Andrew Reid, a soldier of the French and Indian War.

Our author's father was Capt. David E. Moore, for twenty-three years the Attorney for the Commonwealth for Rockbridge County, and a member of the Constitutional Convention, 1850-51. His mother was Miss Elizabeth Harvey, a descendant of Benjamin Borden, and daughter of Matthew Harvey, who at sixteen years of age ran away from home and became a member of "Lee's Legion," participating in the numerous battles in which that distinguished corps took part.

Thus it will be seen that our author is of *martial stock* and a worthy descendant of those who never failed to respond to the call to arms; the youngest of four brothers, one of whom surrendered under General Johnston, the other three at Appomattox, after serving throughout the war. It is safe to say that Virginia furnished to the Confederate service no finer examples of true valor than our author and his three brothers.

HENRY ST. GEORGE TUCKER.

Lexington, Va.,
December 20, 1906.

Edward A. Moore
(1907)

THE STORY OF A CANNONEER UNDER STONEWALL JACKSON

CHAPTER I

WASHINGTON COLLEGE — LEXINGTON — VIRGINIA MILITARY INSTITUTE

At the age of eighteen I was a member of the Junior Class at Washington College at Lexington, Virginia, during the session of 1860-61, and with the rest of the students was more interested in the foreshadowings of that ominous period than in the teachings of the professors. Among our number there were a few from the States farther south who seemed to have been born secessionists, while a large majority of the students were decidedly in favor of the Union.

Our president, the Rev. Dr. George Junkin, who hailed from the North, was heart and soul a Union man, notwithstanding the fact that one of his daughters was the first wife of Major Thomas J. Jackson, who developed into the world-renowned "Stonewall" Jackson. Another daughter was the great Southern poetess, Mrs. Margaret J. Preston, and Dr. Junkin's son, Rev. W. F. Junkin, a most lovable man, became an ardent Southern soldier and a chaplain in the Confederate Army throughout the war.

At the anniversary of the Washington Literary Society, on February 22, 1861, the right of secession was attacked and defended by the participants in the discussion, with no less zeal than they afterward displayed on many bloody battlefields.

We had as a near neighbor the Virginia Military Institute, "The West Point of the South," where scores of her young chivalry were assembled, who were eager to put into practice the subjects taught in their school. Previous to these exciting times not the most kindly feelings, and but little intercourse had existed between the two bodies of young men. The secession element in the College, however, finding more congenial company among the cadets, opened up the way for quite intimate and friendly relations between the two institutions. In January, 1860, the corps of cadets had been ordered by Governor Wise to be present, as a military guard, at the execution of John Brown at Harper's Ferry. After their return more than the usual time was given to the drill; and target-shooting with cannon and small arms was daily practised in our hearing.

Only a small proportion of the citizens of the community favored secession, but they were very aggressive. One afternoon, while a huge Union flag-pole was being raised on the street, which when half-way up snapped and fell to the ground in

pieces, I witnessed a personal encounter between a
cadet and a mechanic (the latter afterward deserted
from our battery during the Gettysburg campaign
in Pennsylvania, his native State), which was
promptly taken up by their respective friends. The
cadets who were present hastened to their barracks
and, joined by their comrades, armed themselves,
and with fixed bayonets came streaming at double-
quick toward the town. They were met at the end
of Main street by their professors, conspicuous
among whom was Colonel Colston on horseback.
He was a native of France and professor of French
at the Institute; he became a major-general in the
Confederate Army and later a general in the Egyp-
tian Army. After considerable persuasion the cadets were induced to return to their barracks.

Instead of the usual Saturday night debates of
the College literary societies, the students either
joined the cadets in their barracks at the Institute
or received them at the College halls to harangue
on the one absorbing topic.

On the top of the main building at the College
was a statue of Washington, and over this statue
some of the students hoisted a palmetto flag. This
greatly incensed our president. He tried, for some
time, but in vain, to have the flag torn down. When
my class went at the usual hour to his room to re-
cite, and before we had taken our seats, he inquired
if the flag was still flying. On being told that it
was, he said, "The class is dismissed; I will never

hear a recitation under a traitor's flag!" And away we went.

Lincoln's proclamation calling for 75,000 men to whip in the seceded States, was immediately followed by the ordinance of secession, and the idea of union was abandoned by all. Recitation-bells no longer sounded; our books were left to gather dust, and forgotten, save only to recall those scenes that filled our minds with the mighty deeds and prowess of such characters as the "Ruling Agamemnon" and his warlike cohorts, and we could almost hear "the terrible clang of striking spears against shields, as it resounded throughout the army."

There was much that seems ludicrous as we recall it now. The youths of the community, imbued with the idea that "cold steel" would play an important part in the conflict, provided themselves with huge bowie-knives, fashioned by our home blacksmith, and with these fierce weapons swinging from their belts were much in evidence. There were already several organized military companies in the county. The Rockbridge Rifles, and a company of cavalry left Lexington April 17, under orders from Governor John Letcher, our townsman, who had just been inaugurated Governor of Virginia, to report at Harper's Ferry. The cavalry company endeavored to make the journey without a halt, and did march the first sixty-four miles in twenty-four hours.

The students formed a company with J. J. White,

professor of Greek, as their captain. Drilling was the occupation of the day; the students having excellent instructors in the cadets and their professors. Our outraged president had set out alone in his private carriage for his former home in the North.

Many of the cadets were called away as drillmasters at camps established in different parts of the South, and later became distinguished officers in the Confederate Army, as did also a large number of the older alumni of the Institute.

The Rockbridge Artillery Company was organized about this time, and, after a fortnight's drilling with the cadet's battery, was ordered to the front, under command of Rev. W. N. Pendleton, rector of the Episcopal Church, and a graduate of West Point, as captain.

The cadets received marching orders, and on that morning, for the first time since his residence in Lexington, Major Jackson was seen in his element. As a professor at the Virginia Military Institute he was remarkable only for strict punctuality and discipline. I, with one of my brothers, had been assigned to his class in Sunday-school, where his regular attendance and earnest manner were equally striking.

It was on a beautiful Sunday morning in May that the cadets received orders to move, and I remember how we were all astonished to see the Christian major, galloping to and fro on a spirited horse, preparing for their departure.

In the arsenal at the Institute were large stores of firearms of old patterns, which were hauled away from time to time to supply the troops. I, with five others of the College company, was detailed as a guard to a convoy of wagons, loaded with these arms, as far as Staunton. We were all about the same size, and with one exception members of the same class. In the first battle of Manassas four of the five present—Charles Bell, William Wilson, William Paxton and Benjamin Bradley—were killed, and William Anderson, now Attorney-General of Virginia, was maimed for life.

There was great opposition on the part of the friends of the students to their going into the service, at any rate in one body, but they grew more and more impatient to be ordered out, and felt decidedly offended at the delay.

Finally, in June, the long-hoped-for orders came. The town was filled with people from far and near, and every one present, old and young, white and black, not only shed tears, but actually sobbed. My father had positively forbidden my going, as his other three sons, older than myself, were already in the field. After this my time was chiefly occupied in drilling militia in different parts of the country. And I am reminded to this day by my friends the daughters of General Pendleton of my apprehensions "lest the war should be over before I should get a trip."

GUN FROM WHICH WAS FIRED THE FIRST HOSTILE CANNON-SHOT
IN THE VALLEY OF VIRGINIA

CHAPTER II

ENTERING THE SERVICE—MY FIRST BATTLE—BATTLE
OF KERNSTOWN

JACKSON's first engagement took place at Hainesville, near Martinsburg, on July 2, one of the Rockbridge Artillery guns firing the first hostile cannon-
shot fired in the Valley of Virginia. This gun is
now in the possession of the Virginia Military Institute, and my brother David fired the shot. Before we knew that Jackson was out of the Valley,
news came of the battle of First Manassas, in which
General Bee conferred upon him and his brigade
the soubriquet of "Stonewall," and by so doing
likened himself to "Homer, who immortalized the
victory won by Achilles."

In this battle the Rockbridge Artillery did splendid execution without losing a man, while the infantry in their rear, and for their support, suffered
dreadfully. The College company alone (now Company I of the Fourth Virginia Regiment) lost seven
killed and many wounded.

In August it was reported that a force of Federal
cavalry was near the White Sulphur Springs, on
their way to Lexington. Numbers of men from the
hills and mountains around gathered at Colliers-
town, a straggling village in the western portion of

the county, and I spent the greater part of the night drilling them in the town-hall, getting news from time to time from the pickets in the mountain-pass. The prospect of meeting so formidable a band had doubtless kept the Federals from even contemplating such an expedition.

The winter passed drearily along, the armies in all directions having only mud to contend with.

Since my failure to leave with the College company it had been my intention to join it the first opportunity; but, hearing it would be disbanded in the spring, I enlisted in the Rockbridge Artillery attached to the Stonewall Brigade, and with about fifty other recruits left Lexington March 10, 1862, to join Jackson, then about thirty miles south of Winchester. Some of us traveled on horseback, and some in farm-wagons secured for the purpose. We did not create the sensation we had anticipated, either on leaving Lexington or along the road; still we had plenty of fun. I remember one of the party —a fellow with a very large chin, as well as cheek— riding up close to a house by the roadside in the door of which stood a woman with a number of children around her, and, taking off his hat, said, "God bless you, madam! May you raise many for the Southern Confederacy."

We spent Saturday afternoon and night in Staunton, and were quartered in a hotel kept by a sour-looking old Frenchman. We were given an abominable supper, the hash especially being a most mys-

terious-looking dish. After retiring to our blankets
on the floor, I heard two of the party, who had par-
taken of some of Bumgardner's mountain dew, discussing the situation generally, and, among other
things, surmising as to the ingredients of the supper's hash, when Winn said, "Bob, I analyzed that
hash. It was made of buttermilk, dried apple, dam-
sons and wool!"

The following day, Sunday, was clear and beautiful. We had about seventy miles to travel along
the Valley turnpike. In passing a stately residence,
on the porch of which the family had assembled,
one of our party raised his hat in salutation. Not
a member of the family took the least notice of the
civility; but a negro girl, who was sweeping off the
pavement in front, flourished her broom around her
head most enthusiastically, which raised a general
shout.

We arrived at Camp Buchanan, a few miles below Mount Jackson, on Monday afternoon. I then,
for the first time since April, 1861, saw my brother
John. How tough and brown he looked! He had
been transferred to the Rockbridge Artillery
shortly before the first battle of Manassas, and with
my brother David belonged to a mess of as interesting young men as I ever knew. Some of them I
have not seen for more than forty years. Mention-
ing their names may serve to recall incidents connected with them: My two brothers, both graduates
of Washington College; Berkeley Minor, a student

of the University of Virginia, a perfect bookworm;
Alex. Boteler, student of the University of Virginia, son of Hon. Alex. Boteler, of West Virginia,
and his two cousins, Henry and Charles Boteler, of
Shepherdstown, West Virginia; Thompson and
Magruder Maury, both clergymen after the war;
Joe Shaner, of Lexington, Virginia, as kind a friend
as I ever had, and who carried my blanket for me
on his off-horse at least one thousand miles; John
M. Gregory, of Charles City County, an A. M. of
the University of Virginia. How distinctly I recall
his large, well-developed head, fair skin and clear
blue eyes; and his voice is as familiar to me as if I
had heard it yesterday. Then the brothers, Walter
and Joe Packard, of the neighborhood of Alexandria, Virginia, sons of the Rev. Dr. Packard, of
the Theological Seminary, and both graduates of
colleges; Frank Preston, of Lexington, graduate of
Washington College, who died soon after the war
while professor of Greek at William and Mary College, a whole-souled and most companionable fellow; William Bolling, of Fauquier County, student
of the University of Virginia; Frank Singleton, of
Kentucky, student of the University of Virginia,
whom William Williamson, another member of the
mess and a graduate of Washington College, pro-
nounced "always a gentleman." Williamson was
quite deaf, and Singleton always, in the gentlest
and most patient way, would repeat for his benefit
anything he failed to hear. Last, and most interest-

ing of all, was George Bedinger, of Sheperdstown, a student of the University of Virginia.

There were men in the company from almost every State in the South, and several from Northern States. Among the latter were two sons of Commodore Porter, of the United States Navy, one of whom went by the name of "Porter-he," from his having gone with Sergeant Paxton to visit some young ladies, and, on their return, being asked how they had enjoyed their visit, the sergeant said, "Oh, splendidly! and Porter, he were very much elated."

Soon after my arrival supper was ready, and I joined the mess in my first meal in camp, and was astonished to see how they relished fat bacon, "flap-jacks" and strong black coffee in big tin cups. The company was abundantly supplied with first-rate tents, many of them captured from the enemy, and everybody seemed to be perfectly at home and happy.

I bunked with my brother John, but there was no sleep for me that first night. There were just enough cornstalks under me for each to be distinctly felt, and the ground between was exceedingly cold. We remained in this camp until the following Friday, when orders came to move.

We first marched about three miles south, or up the Valley, then countermarched, going about twenty miles, and on Sunday, March 23rd, twelve miles farther, which brought us, I thought, and it seemed

to be the general impression, in rather close proximity to the enemy. There having been only a few
skirmishes since Manassas in July, 1861, none of us
dreamed of a battle; but very soon a cannon boomed
two or three miles ahead, then another and another.
The boys said, "That's Chew's battery, under
Ashby."

Pretty soon Chew's battery was answered, and
for the first time I saw and heard a shell burst, high
in the air, leaving a little cloud of white smoke. On
we moved, halting frequently, as the troops were
being deployed in line of battle. Our battery turned
out of the pike and we had not heard a shot for
half an hour. In front of us lay a stretch of half
a mile of level, open ground and beyond this a
wooded hill, for which we seemed to be making.
When half-way across the low ground, as I was
walking by my gun, talking to a comrade at my side,
a shell burst with a terrible crash—it seemed to me
almost on my head. The concussion knocked me to
my knees, and my comrade sprawling on the ground.
We then began to feel that we were "going in," and
a most weakening effect it had on the stomach.

I recall distinctly the sad, solemn feeling produced by seeing the ambulances brought up to the
front; it was entirely too suggestive. Soon we
reached the woods and were ascending the hill along
a little ravine, for a position, when a solid shot
broke the trunnions of one of the guns, thus disabling it; then another, nearly spent, struck a tree

about half-way up and fell nearby. Just after we got to the top of the hill, and within fifty or one hundred yards of the position we were to take, a shell struck the off-wheel horse of my gun and burst. The horse was torn to pieces, and the pieces thrown in every direction. The saddle-horse was also horribly mangled. The leg of the driver, W. H. Byrd, was shot off, as was also the foot of O. P. Gray, who was walking along-side. Both men died that night. A white horse working in the lead looked more like a bay after the catastrophe. To one who had been in the army but five days, and but five minutes under fire, this seemed an awful introduction.

The other guns of the battery had gotten into position before we had cleared up the wreck of our team and put in two new horses. As soon as this was done we pulled up to where the other guns were firing, and passed by a member of the company, John Wallace, horribly torn by a shell, but still alive. On reaching the crest of the hill, which was clear open ground, we got a full view of the enemy's batteries on the hills opposite.

In the woods on our left, and a few hundred yards distant, the infantry were hotly engaged, the small arms keeping up an incessant roar. Neither side seemed to move an inch. From about the Federal batteries in front of us came regiment after regiment of their infantry, marching in line of battle, with the Stars and Stripes flying, to join in the

attack on our infantry, who were not being reinforced at all, as everything but the Fifth Virginia
had been engaged from the first. We did some fine
shooting at their advancing infantry, their batteries
having almost quit firing. The battle had now continued for two or three hours. Now, for the first
time, I heard the keen whistle of the Minie-ball. Our
infantry was being driven back and the Federals
were in close pursuit.

Seeing the day was lost, we were ordered to limber up and leave. Just then a large force of the
enemy came in sight in the woods on our left. The
gunner of the piece nearest them had his piece loaded
with canister, and fired the charge into their ranks
as they crowded through a narrow opening in a
stone fence. One of the guns of the battery, having
several of its horses killed, fell into the hands of
the enemy. About this time the Fifth Virginia
Regiment, which, through some misunderstanding
of orders, had not been engaged, arrived on the
crest of the hill, and I heard General Jackson, as he
rode to their front, direct the men to form in line
and check the enemy. But everything else was now
in full retreat, with Minie-balls to remind us that it
would not do to stop. Running back through the
woods, I passed close by John Wallace as he lay
dying. Night came on opportunely and put an end
to the pursuit, and to the taking of prisoners, though
we lost several hundred men. I afterward heard
Capt. George Junkin, nephew of the Northern col-

lege president, and General Jackson's adjutant, say that he had the exact number of men engaged on our side, and that there were 2,700 in the battle. The enemy's official report gave their number as 8,000. It was dusk when I again found myself on the turnpike, and I followed the few indistinct moving figures in the direction of safety. I stopped for a few minutes near a camp-fire, in a piece of woods, where our infantry halted, and I remember hearing the colored cook of one of their messes asking in piteous tones, over and over again, "Marse George, where's Marse Charles?" No answer was made, but the sorrowful face of the one interrogated was response enough. I got back to the village of New-town, about three miles from the battlefield, where I joined several members of the battery at a hospitable house. Here we were kindly supplied with food, and, as the house was full, were allowed to sleep soundly on the floor. This battle was known as Kernstown.

The Confederate loss was: 80 killed, 375 wounded, 263 captured; total, 718.

Federal loss: 118 killed, 450 wounded, 22 missing; total, 590.

General Jackson was greatly disturbed at being defeated in this battle (claiming that the retreat was premature), and not until it was fully demonstrated by brigade and regimental officers that the infantry yielded only when their ammunition was exhausted did he seem to be reconciled. The effects of it, however, were far-reaching, as some 40,000 Federals in armies for the protection of Washington were prevented from going to join McClellan's advance on Richmond.

In regard to this battle Gen. Jackson wrote to his wife as follows:

"You appear to be much concerned at my attacking on Sunday. I am greatly concerned too . . . and I hope and pray to our Heavenly Father that I may never again be circumstanced as on that day."

In this sentiment many of us fully concurred.

CHAPTER III

THE next dawn brought a raw, gloomy Monday. We found the battery a mile or two from the battle-field, where we lay all day, thinking, of course, the enemy would follow up their victory; but this they showed no inclination to do. On Tuesday we moved a mile or more toward our old camp—Buchanan. On Wednesday, about noon, we reached Cedar Creek, the scene of one of General Early's battles more than two years afterward, 1864. The creek ran through a narrow defile, and, the bridge having been burned, we crossed in single file, on the charred timbers, still clinging together and resting on the surface of the water. Just here, for the first time since Kernstown, the Federal cavalry attacked the rear of our column, and the news and commotion reached my part of the line when I was half-across the stream. The man immediately in front of me, being in too much of a hurry to follow the file on the bridge-planks, jumped frantically into the stream. He was fished out of the cold waters, shoulder deep, on the bayonets of the infantry on the timbers.

We found our wagons awaiting us on top of a high hill beyond, and went into camp about noon, to get up a whole meal, to which we thought we could do full justice. But, alas! alas! About the time the beans were done, and each had his share in a tin plate or cup, "bang!" went a cannon on the opposite hill, and the shell screamed over our heads. My gun being a rifled piece, was ordered to hitch up and go into position, and my appetite was gone. Turning to my brother, I said, "John, I don't want these beans!" My friend Bedinger gave me a home-made biscuit, which I ate as I followed the gun. We moved out and across the road with two guns, and took position one hundred yards nearer the enemy. The guns were unlimbered and loaded just in time to fire at a column of the enemy's cavalry which had started down the opposite hill at a gallop. The guns were discharged simultaneously, and the two shells burst in the head of their column, and by the time the smoke and dust had cleared up that squadron of cavalry was invisible. This check gave the wagons and troops time to get in marching order, and after firing a few more rounds we followed.

As we drove into the road again, I saw several infantrymen lying, horribly torn by shells, and the clothes of one of them on fire. I afterward heard amusing accounts of the exit of the rest of the company from this camp. Quartermaster "John D." had his teams at a full trot, with the steam flying from the still hot camp-kettles as they rocked to and fro on the tops of the wagons. In a day or two we were again in Camp Buchanan, and pitched our tents on their old sites and kindled our fires with the old embers. Here more additions were made to the company, among them R. E. Lee, Jr., son of the General; Arthur Robinson, of Baltimore, and Edward Hyde, of Alexandria. After a few nights' rest and one or two square meals everything was as gay as ever.

An hour or two each day was spent in going through the artillery manual. Every morning we heard the strong, clear voice of an infantry officer drilling his men, which I learned was the voice of our cousin, James Allen, colonel of the Second Virginia Regiment. He was at least half a mile distant. About the fourth or fifth day after our return to camp we were ordered out to meet the enemy, and moved a few miles in their direction, but were relieved on learning that it was a false alarm, and counter-marched to the same camp. When we went to the wagons for our cooking utensils, etc., my heavy double blanket, brought from home, had been lost, which made the ground seem colder and the stalks rougher. With me the nights, until bedtime, were pleasant enough. There were some good voices in the company, two or three in our mess; Bedinger and his cousin, Alec Boteler, both sang well, but Boteler stammered badly when talking, and Bedinger kept him in a rage half the time mocking him, frequently advising him to go

back home and learn to talk. Still they were bed-
fellows and devoted friends. I feel as if I could
hear Bedinger now, as he shifted around the fire, to
keep out of the smoke, singing:

"Though the world may call me gay, yet my feelings I smother,
Oh! thou hast been the cause of this anguish—my mother."

.   .   .   .

A thing that I was very slow to learn was to sit
on the ground with any comfort; and a log or a
fence, for a few minutes' rest, was a thing of joy.
Then the smoke from the camp-fires almost suffo-
cated me, and always seemed to blow toward me,
though each of the others thought himself the favored one. But the worst part of the twenty-four
hours was from bedtime till daylight, half-awake
and half-asleep and half-frozen. I was, since
Kernstown, having that battle all over and over
again.

I noticed a thing in this camp (it being the first
winter of the war), in which experience and necessity afterward made a great change. The soldiers,
not being accustomed to fires out-of-doors, frequently had either the tails of their overcoats
burned off, or big holes or scorched places in their
pantaloons.

Since Jackson's late reverse, more troops being
needed, the militia had been ordered out, and the
contingent from Rockbridge County was encamped
a few miles in rear of us. I got permission from
our captain to go to see them and hear the news from

home. Among them were several merchants of Lexington, and steady old farmers from the county. They were much impressed with the accounts of the battle and spoke very solemnly of war. I had ridden Sergeant Baxter McCorkle's horse, and, on my return, soon after passing through Mt. Jackson, overtook Bedinger and Charley Boteler, with a canteen of French brandy which a surgeon-friend in town had given them. As a return for a drink, I asked Bedinger to ride a piece on my horse, which, for some time, he declined to do, but finally said, "All right; get down." He had scarcely gotten into the saddle before he plied the horse with hat and heels, and away he went down the road at full speed and disappeared in the distance.

This was more kindness than I had intended, but it afforded a good laugh. Boteler and the brandy followed the horseman, and I turned in and spent the night with the College company, quartered close by as a guard to General Jackson's headquarters. I got back to camp the next afternoon, Sunday. McCorkle had just found his horse, still saddled and bridled, grazing in a wheat-field.

From Camp Buchanan we fell back to Rude's Hill, four miles above Mt. Jackson and overlooking the Shenandoah River. About once in three days our two Parrott guns, to one of which I belonged, were sent down to General Ashby, some ten miles, for picket service to supply the place of Chew's battery, which exhausted its ammunition in daily skirmishes with the enemy. Ashby himself was always there; and an agreeable, unpretending gentleman he was. His complexion was very dark and his hair and beard as black as a raven. He was always in motion, mounted on one of his three superb stallions, one of which was coal-black, another a chestnut sorrel, and the third white. On our first trip we had a lively cannonade, and the white horse in our team, still bearing the stains of blood from the Kernstown carnage, reared and plunged furiously during the firing. The Federal skirmish line was about a mile off, near the edge of some woods, and at that distance looked very harmless; but when I looked at them through General Ashby's field-glass it made them look so large, and brought them so close, that it startled me. There was a fence intervening, and, on giving the glass a slight jar, I imagined they jumped the fence; I preferred looking at them with the naked eye. Bob Lee volunteered to go with us another day (he belonged to another detachment). He seemed to enjoy the sport much. He had not been at Kernstown, and I thought if he had, possibly he would have felt more as did I and the white horse.

On our way down on another expedition, hearing the enemy were driving in our pickets, and that we would probably have some lively work and running, I left my blanket—a blue one I had recently borrowed—at the house of a mulatto woman by the roadside, and told her I would call for it as we came back. We returned soon, but the woman, learning that a battle was impending, had locked up and gone. This blanket was my only wrap during the chilly nights, so I must have it. The guns had gone on. As I stood deliberating as to what I should do, General Ashby came riding by. I told him my predicament and asked, "Shall I get in and get it?" He said, "Yes, certainly." With the help of an axe I soon had a window-sash out and my blanket in my possession. From these frequent picket excursions I got the name of "Veteran." My friend Bolling generously offered to go as my substitute on one expedition, but the Captain, seeing our two detachments were being overworked, had all relieved and sent other detachments with our guns.

From Rude's Hill about fifty of us recruits were detailed to go to Harrisonburg—Lieutenant Graham in command—to guard prisoners. The prisoners were quartered in the courthouse. Among them were a number of Dunkards from the surrounding country, whose creed was "No fight." I was appointed corporal, the only promotion I was honored with during the war, and that only for the detailed service. Here we spent a week or ten days, pleasantly, with good fare and quarters. Things continued quiet at the front during this time.

The enemy again advanced, and quite a lively calvary skirmish was had from Mt. Jackson to the bridge across the Shenandoah. The enemy tried hard to keep our men from burning this bridge, and in the fray Ashby's white horse was mortally wounded under him and his own life saved by the daring interposition of one of his men. His horse lived to carry him out, but fell dead as soon as he had accomplished it; and, after his death, every hair was pulled from his tail by Ashby's men as mementoes of the occasion.

Jackson fell back slowly, and, on reaching Harrisonburg, to our dismay, the head of the column filed to the left, on the road leading toward the Blue Ridge, thus disclosing the fact that the Valley was to be given up a prey to the enemy. Gloom was seen on every face at feeling that our homes were forsaken. We carried our prisoners along, and a miserable-looking set the poor Dunkards were, with their long beards and solemn eyes. A little fun, though, we would have. Every mile or so, and at every cross-road, a sign-post was stuck up, "Keezletown Road, 2 miles," and of every countryman or darky along the way some wag would inquire the distance to Keezletown, and if he thought we could get there before night.

By dawn next morning we were again on the march. I have recalled this early dawn oftener, I am sure, than any other of my whole life. Our road lay along the edge of a forest, occasionally winding in and out of it. At the more open places we could see the Blue Ridge in the near distance. During the night a slight shower had moistened the earth and leaves, so that our steps, and even the wheels of the artillery, were scarcely heard. Here and there on the roadside was the home of a soldier, in which he had just passed probably his last night. I distinctly recall now the sobs of a wife or mother as she moved about, preparing a meal for her husband or son, and the thoughts it gave rise to. Very possibly it helped also to remind us that we had left camp that morning without any breakfast ourselves. At any rate, I told my friend, Joe McCalpin, who was quite too modest a man to forage, and face a strange family in quest of a meal, that if he would put himself in my charge I would promise him a good breakfast.

In a few miles we reached McGaheysville, a quiet, comfortable little village away off in the hills. The sun was now up, and now was the time and this the place. A short distance up a cross-street I saw a motherly-looking old lady standing at her gate, watching the passing troops. Said I, "Mac, there's the place." We approached, and I announced the object of our visit. She said, "Breakfast is just ready. Walk in, sit down at the table, and make yourselves at home. A breakfast it was—fresh eggs, white light biscuit and other toothsome articles. A man of about forty-five years—a boarder—remarked, at the table, "The war has not cost me the loss of an hour's sleep." The good mother said, with a quavering tone of voice, "*I* have sons in the army."

CHAPTER IV

SWIFT RUN GAP—REORGANIZATION OF THE BATTERY
— WADING IN THE MUD — CROSSING AND
RECROSSING THE BLUE RIDGE — BATTLE OF
MCDOWELL—RETURN TO THE VALLEY

WE reached the south branch of the Shenandoah about noon, crossed on a bridge, and that night camped in Swift Run Gap. Our detail was separated from the battery and I, therefore, not with my own mess. We occupied a low, flat piece of ground with a creek alongside and about forty yards from the tent in which I stayed. The prisoners were in a barn a quarter of a mile distant. Here we had most wretched weather, real winter again, rain or snow almost all the time. One night about midnight I was awakened by hearing a horse splashing through water just outside of the tent and a voice calling to the inmates to get out of the flood. The horse was backed half into the tent-door, and, one by one, my companions left me. My bunk was on a little rise. I put my hand out—into the water. I determined, however, to stay as long as I could, and was soon asleep, which showed that I was becoming a soldier—in one important respect at least. By daylight, the flood having subsided, I was able to reach a fence and "coon it" to a hill above.

While in this camp, as the time had expired for which most of the soldiers enlisted, the army was reorganized. The battery having more men than was a quota for one company, the last recruits were required to enlist in other companies or to exchange with older members who wished to change. Thus some of our most interesting members left us, to join other commands, and the number of our guns was reduced from eight to six. The prisoners were now disposed of, and I returned to my old mess. After spending about ten days in this wretched camp we marched again, following the Shenandoah River along the base of the mountains toward Port Republic. After such weather, the dirt-roads were, of course, almost bottomless. The wagons monopolized them during the day, so we had to wait until they were out of the way. When they halted for the night, we took the mud. The depth of it was nearly up to my knees and frequently over them. The bushes on the sides of the road, and the darkness, compelled us to wade right in. Here was swearing and growling, "Flanders and Flounders." An infantryman was cursing Stonewall most eloquently, when the old Christian rode by, and, hearing him, said, in his short way, "It's for your own good, sir!" The wagons could make only six miles during the day, and, by traveling this distance after night, we reached them about nine o'clock. We would then build fires, get our cooking utensils, and cook our suppers, and, by the light of the fires, see

our muddy condition and try to dry off before retiring to the ground. We engaged in this sort of
warfare for three days, when we reached Port Republic, eighteen miles from our starting-point and
about the same distance from Staunton. Our movements, or rather Jackson's, had entirely bewildered
us as to his intentions.

While we were at Swift Run, Ewell's division,
having been brought from the army around Richmond, was encamped just across the mountain opposite us. We remained at Port Republic several
days. Our company was convenient to a comfortable farmhouse, where hot apple turnovers were
constantly on sale. Our hopes for remaining in the
Valley were again blasted when the wagons moved
out on the Brown's Gap road and we followed
across the Blue Ridge, making our exit from the
pass a few miles north of Mechum's River, which
we reached about noon of the following day.

There had been a good deal of cutting at each
other among the members of the company who
hailed from different sides of the Blue Ridge—
"Tuckahoes" and "Cohees," as they are provin-
cially called. "Lit" Macon, formerly sheriff of
Albemarle County, an incessant talker, had given
us glowing accounts of the treatment we would receive "on t'other side." "Jam puffs, jam puffs!"
Joe Shaner and I, having something of a turn for
investigating the resources of a new country, took
the first opportunity of testing Macon's promised

land. We selected a fine-looking house, and, approaching it, made known our wants to a young lady. She left us standing outside of the yard, we supposed to cool off while she made ready for our entertainment in the house. In this we were mistaken; for, after a long time, she returned and handed us, through the fence, some cold corn-bread and bacon. This and similar experiences by others gave us ample means to tease Macon about the grand things we were to see and enjoy "on t'other side."

We were now much puzzled as to the meaning of this "wiring in and wiring out," as we had turned to the right on crossing the mountain and taken the road toward Staunton. To our astonishment we recrossed the mountain, from the top of which we again gazed on that grand old Valley, and felt that our homes might still be ours. A mile or two from the mountain lay the quiet little village of Waynesboro, where we arrived about noon. As I was passing along the main street, somewhat in advance of the battery, Frank Preston came running out of one of the houses—the Waddells'—and, with his usual take-no-excuse style, dragged me in to face a family of the prettiest girls in Virginia. I was immediately taken to the dining-room, where were "jam puffs" sure enough, and the beautiful Miss Nettie to divide my attention.

The next day we camped near Staunton and remained a day. Conjecturing now as to Jackson's program was wild, so we concluded to let him have

his own way. The cadets of the Virginia Military
Institute, most of whom were boys under seventeen,
had, in this emergency, been ordered to the field,
and joined the line of march as we passed through
Staunton, and the young ladies of that place made
them the heroes of the army, to the disgust of the
"Veterans" of the old Stonewall Brigade. Our
course was now westward, and Milroy, who was too
strong for General Ed. Johnson in the Alleghanies,
was the object. About twenty miles west of Staunton was the home of a young lady friend, and, on
learning that our road lay within four miles of it,
I determined at least to try to see her. Sergeant
Clem. Fishburne, who was related to the family,
expected to go with me, but at the last moment gave
it up, so I went alone. To my very great disappointment she was not at home, but her sisters entertained me nicely with music, etc., and filled my
haversack before I left. Just before starting off in
the afternoon I learned that cannonading had been
heard toward the front. When a mile or two on
my way a passing cavalryman, a stranger to me,
kindly offered to carry my overcoat, which he did,
and left it with the battery.

The battery had marched about fifteen miles
after I had left it, so I had to retrace my four miles,
then travel the fifteen, crossing two mountains. I
must have walked at least five miles an hour, as I
reached the company before sundown. They had
gone into camp. My brother John, and Frank

Preston, seeing me approach, came out to meet me, and told me how excessively uneasy they had been about me all day. A battle had been fought and they had expected to be called on every moment, and, "Suppose we *had* gone in, and you off foraging!" How penitent I felt, and at the same time how grateful for having two such anxious guardians! While expressing this deep interest they each kept an eye on my full haversack. "Well," said I, "I have some pabulum here; let's go to the mess and give them a snack." They said, "That little bit wouldn't be a drop in the bucket with all that mess; let's just go down yonder to the branch and have one real good old-fashioned repast." So off we went to the branch, and by the time they were through congratulating me on getting back before the battery had "gotten into it," my haversack was empty. The battle had been fought by Johnson's division, the enemy whipped and put to flight. The next day we started in pursuit, passing through McDowell, a village in Highland County, and near this village the fight had occurred. The ground was too rough and broken for the effective use of artillery, so the work was done by the infantry on both sides. This was the first opportunity that many of us had had of seeing a battlefield the day after the battle. The ghastly faces of the dead made a sickening and lasting impression; but I hoped I did not look as pale as did some of the young cadets, who proved gallant enough afterward. We continued the pursuit a day or two through that wild mount-tainous country, but Milroy stopped only once after his defeat, for a skirmish. In a meadow and near the roadside stood a deserted cabin, which had been struck several times during the skirmish by shells. I went inside of it, to see what a shell could do. Three had penetrated the outer wall and burst in the house, and I counted twenty-seven holes made through the frame partition by the fragments. Being an artilleryman, and therefore to be exposed to missiles of that kind, I concluded that my chances for surviving the war were extremely slim.

While on this expedition an amusing incident occurred in our mess. There belonged to it quite a character. He was not considered a pretty boy, and tried to get even with the world by taking good care of himself. We had halted one morning to cook several days' rations, and a large pile of bread was placed near the fire, of which we were to eat our breakfast and the rest was to be divided among us. He came, we thought, too often to the pile, and helped himself bountifully; he would return to his seat on his blanket, and one or two of us saw, or thought we saw him conceal pieces of bread under it. Nothing was said at the time, but after he had gone away Bolling, Packard and I concluded to examine his haversack, which looked very fat. In it we found about half a gallon of rye for coffee, a hock of bacon, a number of home-made buttered biscuit, a hen-egg and a goose-egg, besides more

than his share of camp rations. Here was our
chance to teach a Christian man in an agreeable way
that he should not appropriate more than his share
of the rations without the consent of the mess, so
we set to and ate heartily of his good stores, and in
their place put, for ballast, a river-jack that weighed
about two pounds. He carried the stone for two
days before he ate down to it, and, when he did, was
mad enough to eat it. We then told him what we
had done and why; but thought he had hidden
enough under his blanket to carry him through the
campaign.

Before leaving the Valley we had observed de-
cided evidences of spring; but here it was like midwinter—not a bud nor blade of grass to be seen.
Milroy was now out of reach, so we retraced our
steps. On getting out of the mountains we bore to
the left of Staunton in the direction of Harrisonburg, twenty-five miles northeast of the former.
After the bleak mountains, with their leafless trees,
the old Valley looked like Paradise. The cherry-
and peach-trees were loaded with bloom, the fields
covered with rank clover, and how our weary
horses did revel in it! We camped the first night
in a beautiful meadow, and soon after settling down
I borrowed Sergeant Gregory's one-eyed horse to
go foraging on. I was very successful; I got supper at a comfortable Dutch house, and at it and one
or two others I bought myself and the mess rich.
As I was returning to camp after night with a ham

of bacon between me and the pommel of the saddle, a bucket of butter on one arm, a kerchief of pies on the other, and chickens swung across behind, my one-eyed horse stumbled and fell forward about ten feet with his nose to the ground. I let him take care of himself while I took care of my provisions. When he recovered his feet and started, I do not think a single one of my possessions had slipped an inch.

CHAPTER V

BRIDGEWATER — LURAY VALLEY — FRONT ROYAL —
FOLLOWING GENERAL BANKS—NIGHT MARCH—
BATTLE OF WINCHESTER—BANK'S RETREAT

THE next day we who were on foot crossed the Shenandoah on a bridge made of wagons standing side by side, with tongues up-stream, and boards extending from one wagon to another. We reached Bridgewater about four P. M. It was a place of which I had never heard, and a beautiful village it proved to be, buried in trees and flowers. From Bridgewater we went to Harrisonburg, and then on our old familiar and beaten path—the Valley pike to New Market. Thence obliquely to the right, crossing the Massanutten Mountain into Luray Valley. During the Milroy campaign Ewell had crossed into the Valley, and we now followed his division, which was several miles in advance. Banks was in command of the Union force in the Valley, with his base at Winchester and detachments of his army at Strasburg, eighteen miles southwest, and at Front Royal, about the same distance in the Luray Valley. So the latter place was to be attacked first. About three P. M. the following day cannonading was heard on ahead, and, after a sharp fight,

Ewell carried the day. We arrived about sundown, after it was all over. In this battle the First Maryland Regiment (Confederate) had met the First Maryland (Federal) and captured the whole regiment. Several members of our battery had brothers or other relatives in the Maryland (Confederate) regiment, whom they now met for the first time since going into service. Next day we moved toward Middletown on the Valley pike, and midway between Winchester and Strasburg.

Jackson's rapid movements seemed to have taken the enemy entirely by surprise, and we struck their divided forces piecemeal, and even after the Front Royal affair their troops at Strasburg, consisting chiefly of cavalry, had not moved. Two of our guns were sent on with the Louisiana Tigers, to intercept them at Middletown. The guns were posted about one hundred and fifty yards from the road, and the Tigers strung along behind a stone fence on the roadside. Everything was in readiness when the enemy came in sight. They wavered for a time, some trying to pass around, but, being pushed from behind, there was no alternative. Most of them tried to run the gauntlet; few, however, got through. As the rest of us came up we met a number of prisoners on horseback. They had been riding at a run for nine miles on the pike in a cloud of white dust. Many of them were hatless, some had sabre-cuts on their heads and streams of blood were coursing down through the dust on their faces. Among them was a woman wearing a short red skirt and mounted on a tall horse.

Confined in a churchyard in the village were two or three hundred prisoners. As we were passing by them an old negro cook, belonging to the Alleghany Rough Battery of our brigade, ran over to the fence and gave them a hearty greeting, said he was delighted to see them "thar," and that we would catch all the rest of them before they got back home. Bank's main force was at Winchester, and thither we directed our course.

Newtown was the next village, and there we had another skirmish, our artillery being at one end of the town and the enemy's at the opposite. In this encounter two members of our battery, Calvin Dold and George Ginger, were wounded. There was great rejoicing among the people to see us back again and to be once more free from Northern soldiers. As the troops were passing through Newtown a very portly old lady came running out on her porch, and, spreading her arms wide, called out, "All of you run here and kiss me!"

Our captures were not confined to men and horses, but army stores of all kinds. From a butler's wagon we passed, William Bolling secured a whole barrel of ginger cakes, which he placed in our ambulance at the rear of the battery. Word was passed along the line and soon a large funeral procession was in its wake devouring ginger cakes.

Night soon set in, and a long, weary night it was;

the most trying I ever passed, in war or out of it. From dark till daylight we did not advance more than four miles. Step by step we moved along, halting for five minutes; then on a few steps and halt again. About ten o'clock we passed by a house rather below the roadside, on the porch of which lay several dead Yankees, a light shining on their ghastly faces. Occasionally we were startled by the sharp report of a rifle, followed in quick succession by others; then all as quiet as the grave. Sometimes, when a longer halt was made, we would endeavor to steal a few moments' sleep, for want of which it was hard to stand up. By the time a blanket was unrolled, the column was astir again, and so it continued throughout the long, dreary hours of the night.

At last morning broke, clear and beautiful, finding us about two miles from Winchester. After moving on for perhaps half a mile, we filed to the left. All indications were that a battle was imminent, Banks evidently intending to make one more effort. The sun was up, and never shone on a prettier country nor a lovelier May morning. Along our route was a brigade of Louisiana troops under the command of Gen. Dick Taylor, of Ewell's division. They were in line of battle in a ravine, and as we were passing by them several shells came screaming close over our heads and burst just beyond. I heard a colonel chiding his men for dodging, one of whom called out, in reply, "Colonel, lead us up to where we can get at them and then we won't dodge !" We passed on, bearing to the left and in the direction from which the shells came. General Jackson ordered us to take position on the hill just in front. The ground was covered with clover, and as we reached the crest we were met by a volley of musketry from a line of infantry behind a stone fence about two hundred yards distant.

My gun was one of the last to get into position, coming up on the left. I was assigned the position of No. 2, Jim Ford No. 1. The Minie-balls were now flying fast by our heads, through the clover and everywhere. A charge of powder was handed me, which I put into the muzzle of the gun. In a rifled gun this should have been rammed home first, but No. 1 said, "Put in your shell and let one ram do. Hear those Minies?" I heard them and adopted the suggestion; the consequence was, the charge stopped half-way down and there it stuck, and the gun was thereby rendered unavailable. This was not very disagreeable, even from a patriotic point of view, as we could do but little good shooting at infantry behind a stone fence. On going about fifty yards to the rear, I came up with my friend and messmate, Gregory, who was being carried by several comrades. A Minie-ball had gone through his left arm into his breast and almost through his body, lodging in the right side of his back. Still he recovered, and was a captain of ordnance at the surrender, and two years ago I visited him at his own home in California. As my train stopped at his depot, and I saw a portly old gentleman with a long white beard coming to meet it, I thought of the youth I remembered, and said, "Can that be Gregory?"

Then came Frank Preston with his arm shattered, which had to be amputated at the shoulder. I helped to carry Gregory to a barn one hundred and fifty yards in the rear, and there lay Bob McKim, of Baltimore, another member of the company, shot through the head and dying. Also my messmate, Wash. Stuart, who had recently joined the battery. A ball had struck him just below the cheek-bone, and, passing through the mouth, came out on the opposite side of his face, breaking out most of his jaw-teeth. Then came my brother John with a stream of blood running from the top of his head, and, dividing at the forehead, trickled in all directions down his face. My brother David was also slightly wounded on the arm by a piece of shell. By this time the Louisianians had been "led up to where they could get at them," and gotten them on the run. As one of our guns was being put into position a gate-post interfered and was jammed between a wheel and the tongue. In response to Capt. Poague's request for volunteers to cut it down, Cannoneer Whitt promptly undertook and completed the task, under a constant hail of bullets from the sharp-shooters behind the stone-wall.

In this battle, known as First Winchester, two of

CAPT. W. T. POAGUE

the battery were killed and twelve or fourteen
wounded. The fighting was soon over and became
a chase. My gun being *hors de combat*, I remained
awhile with the wounded, so did not witness the first
wild enthusiasm of the Winchester people as our
men drove the enemy through the streets, but heard
that the ladies could not be kept indoors. Our battery did itself credit on this occasion. I will quote
from Gen. Dick Taylor's book, entitled "Destruction and Reconstruction": "Jackson was on the
pike and near him were several regiments lying
down for shelter, as the fire from the ridge was
heavy and searching. A Virginian battery, the
Rockbridge Artillery, was fighting at great disadvantage, and already much cut up. Poetic authority asserts that 'Old Virginny never tires,' and the
conduct of this battery justified the assertion of the
muses. With scarce a leg or wheel for man and
horse, gun or caisson, to stand on, it continued to
hammer away at the crushing fire above." And
further on in the same narrative he says, "Meanwhile, the Rockbridge Battery held on manfully
and engaged the enemy's attention." Dr. Dabney's
"Life of Stonewall Jackson," page 377, says:
"Just at this moment General Jackson rode forward, followed by two field-officers, to the very
crest of the hill, and, amidst a perfect shower of
balls reconnoitred the whole position.   .   .   .
He saw them posting another battery, with which
they hoped to enfilade the ground occupied by the

guns of Poague; and nearer to his left front a body of riflemen were just seizing a position behind a stone fence when they poured a galling fire upon the gunners and struck down many men and horses. Here this gallant battery stood its ground, sometimes almost silenced, yet never yielding an inch. After a time they changed their front to the left, and while a part of their guns replied to the opposing battery the remainder shattered the stone fence, which sheltered the Federal infantry, with solid shot and raked it with canister."

In one of the hospitals I saw Jim ("Red") Jordan, an old schoolmate and member of the Alleghany Roughs, with his arm and shoulder horribly mangled by a shell. He had beautiful brown eyes, and, as I came into the room where he lay tossing on his bed, he opened them for a moment and called my name, but again fell back delirious, and soon afterward died.

The chase was now over, and the town full of soldiers and officers, especially the latter. I was invited by John Williams, better known as "Johnny," to spend the night at his home, a home renowned even in hospitable Winchester for its hospitality. He had many more intimate friends than I, and the house was full. Still I thought I received more attention and kindness than even the officers. I was given a choice room all to myself, and never shall I forget the impression made by the sight of that clean, snow-white bed, the first I had seen since taking up arms for my country, which already seemed to me a lifetime. I thought I must lie awake a while, in order to take in the situation, then go gradually to sleep, realizing that to no rude alarm was I to hearken, and once or twice during the night to wake up and realize it again. But, alas! my plans were all to no purpose; for, after the continual marching and the vigils of the previous night, I was asleep the moment my head touched the pillow, nor moved a muscle till breakfast was announced next morning.

CHAPTER VI

CAPTURING FEDERAL CAVALRY — CHARLESTOWN — EXTRAORDINARY MARCH

AFTER camping for a day or two about three miles below Winchester we marched again toward Harper's Ferry, thirty miles below. Four of the six guns of the battery were sent in advance with the infantry of the brigade; the other two guns, to one of which I belonged, coming on leisurely in the rear. As we approached Charlestown, seated on the limbers and caissons, we saw three or four of our cavalrymen coming at full speed along a road on our left, which joined the road we were on, making an acute angle at the end of the main street. They announced "Yankee cavalry" as they passed and disappeared into the town. In a moment the Federals were within one hundred yards of us. We had no officer, except Sergeant Jordan, but we needed none. Instantly every man was on his feet, the guns unlimbered, and, by the time the muzzles were in the right direction, No. 5 handed me a charge of canister, No. 1 standing ready to ram. Before I put the charge into the gun the enemy had come to a halt within eighty yards of us, and their commanding officer drew and waved a white handkerchief. We, afraid to leave our guns lest they

62

should escape or turn the tables on us, after some time prevailed on our straggling cavalry, who had halted around the turn, to ride forward and take them. There were seventeen Federals, well-mounted and equipped. Our cavalry claimed all the spoils, and I heard afterward most of the credit, too. We got four of the horses, one of which, under various sergeants and corporals, and by the name of "Fizzle,' became quite a celebrity.

Delighted with our success and gallantry, we again mounted our caissons and entered the town at a trot. The people had been under Northern rule for a long time, and were rejoiced to greet their friends. I heard a very old lady say to a little girl, as we drove by, "Oh, dear! if your father was just here, to see this!" The young ladies were standing on the sides of the streets, and, as our guns rattled by, would reach out to hand us some of the dainties from their baskets; but we had had plenty, so they could not reach far enough. The excitement over, we went into camp in a pretty piece of woods two miles below the town and six from Harper's Ferry. Here we spent several days pleasantly.

Mayor Middleton, of our town, Lexington, had followed us with a wagonload of boxes of edibles from home. So many of the company had been wounded or left behind that the rest of us had a double share. Gregory's box, which Middleton brought from the railroad, contained a jar of delicious pickle. I had never relished it before, but camp-life had created a craving for it that seemed insatiable. The cows of the neighborhood seemed to have a curiosity to see us, and would stroll around the camp and stand kindly till a canteen could be filled with rich milk, which could soon be cooled in a convenient spring. Just outside of Charlestown lived the Ransons, who had formerly lived near Lexington and were great friends of my father's family. I called to see them. "Buck," the second son, was then about fifteen and chafing to go into the army. I took a clean shave with his razor, which he used daily to encourage his beard and shorten his stay in Jericho. He treated me to a flowing goblet of champagne left by the Federal officers in their haste, and gave me a lead-colored knit jacket, with a blue border, in which I felt quite fine, and wore through the rest of the campaign. It was known in the mess as my "Josey." "Buck" eventually succeeded in getting in, and now bears the scars of three saber-cuts on his head.

It was raining the day we broke camp and started toward Winchester, but our march was enlivened by the addition of a new recruit in the person of Steve Dandridge. He was about sixteen and had just come from the Virginia Military Institute, where he had been sent to be kept out of the army. He wore a cadet-cap which came well over the eyes and nose, and left a mass of brown, curly hair unprotected on the back of his head. His joy at being "mustered in" was irrepressible. He had no ear

for music, was really "too good-natured to strike
a tune," but the songs he tried to sing would have
made a "dog laugh." Within an hour after his
arrival he was on intimate terms with everybody
and knew and called us all by our first names.

The march of this day was one of the noted ones
of the war. Our battery traveled about thirty-five
miles, and the infantry of the brigade, being camped
within a mile of Harper's Ferry, made more than
forty miles through rain and mud. The cause of
this haste was soon revealed. General Fremont,
with a large army, was moving rapidly from the
north to cut us off, and was already nearer our base
than we were, while General Shields, with another
large force, was pushing from the southeast, having
also the advantage of us in distance, and trying to
unite with Fremont, and General McDowell with
20,000 men was at Fredericksburg. The roads on
which the three armies were marching concentrated
at Strasburg, and Jackson was the first to get there.
Two of our guns were put in position on a fortified
hill near the town, from which I could see the pickets of both the opposing armies on their respective
roads and numbers of our stragglers still following
on behind us, between the two. Many of our officers had collected around our guns with their field-
glasses, and, at the suggestion of one of them, we
fired a few rounds at the enemy's videttes "to hurry
up our stragglers."

The next day, when near the village of Edinburg, a squadron of our cavalry, under command of General Munford, was badly stampeded by a charge of Federal cavalry. Suddenly some of these men and horses without riders came dashing through our battery, apparently blind to objects in their front. One of our company was knocked down by the knees of a flying horse, and, as the horse was making his next leap toward him, his bridle was seized by a driver and the horse almost doubled up and brought to a standstill. This was the only time I ever heard a field-officer upbraided by privates; but one of the officers got ample abuse from us on that occasion.

I had now again, since Winchester, been assigned to a Parrott gun, and it, with another, was ordered into position on the left of the road. The Federals soon opened on us with two guns occupying an unfavorable position considerably below us. The gunner of my piece was J. P. Smith, who afterward became an aide on General Jackson's staff, and was with him when he received his death-wound at Chancellorsville. One of the guns firing at us could not, for some time, be accurately located, owing to some small trees, etc., which intervened, so the other gun received most of our attention. Finally, I marked the hidden one exactly, beyond a small tree, from the puff of smoke when it fired. I then asked J. P., as we called him, to let me try a shot at it, to which he kindly assented. I got a first-rate aim and ordered "Fire!" The enemy's gun did not fire again, though its companion continued for some time. I have often wished to know what damage I did them.

The confusion of the stampede being over, the line of march was quietly resumed for several miles, until we reached "The Narrows," where we again went into position. I had taken a seat by the roadside and was chatting with a companion while the guns drove out into a field to prepare for action, and, as I could see the ground toward the enemy, I knew that I had ample time to get to my post before being needed. When getting out the accouterments the priming-wire could not be found. I being No. 3 was, of course, responsible for it. I heard Captain Poague, on being informed who No. 3 was, shout, "Ned Moore, where is that priming-wire?" I replied, "It is in the limber-chest where it belongs." There were a good many people around, and I did not wish it to appear that I had misplaced my little priming-wire in the excitement of covering Stonewall's retreat. The captain yelled, as I thought unnecessarily, "It isn't there!" I, in the same tone, replied, "It is there, and I will get it!" So off I hurried, and, to my delight, there it was in its proper place, and I brought it forth with no small flourish and triumph.

After waiting here for a reasonable time, and no foe appearing, we followed on in rear of the column without further molestation or incident that I can now recall. We reached Harrisonburg after a few days' marching.

CHAPTER VII

GENERAL JACKSON NARROWLY ESCAPES BEING CAP-
TURED AT PORT REPUBLIC—CONTEST BETWEEN
CONFEDERATES AND FEDERALS FOR BRIDGE OVER
SHENANDOAH

THE College company had as cook a very black
negro boy named Pete, who through all this marching had carried, on a baggage-wagon, a small game
rooster which he named "Ashby" and which he told
me had whipped every chicken from Harrisonburg
to Winchester and back again. At last poor Ashby
met defeat, and Pete consigned him to the pot, saying, "No chicken dat kin be whipped shall go 'long
wid Jackson's headquarters." At Harrisonburg we
turned to the left again, but this time obliquely, in
the direction of Port Republic, twenty miles distant.
We went into camp on Saturday evening, June 7,
about one mile from Port Republic and on the north
side of the Shenandoah. Shields had kept his army
on the south side of this stream and had been moving parallel with us during our retreat. Jackson's
division was in advance. Instead of going into
camp, I, with two messmates, Bolling and Walter
Packard, diverged to a log-house for supper. The
man of the house was quiet; his wife did the talk-

ing, and a great deal of it. She flatly refused us a
bite to eat, but, on stating the case to her, she consented to let us have some bread and milk. Seated
around an unset dining-table we began divesting
ourselves of our knapsacks. She said, "Just keep
your baggage on; you can eat a bite and go." We
told her we could eat faster unharnessed. She
sliced a loaf of bread as sad as beeswax, one she
had had on hand for perhaps a week, and gave us
each a bowl of sour milk, all the while reminding
us to make our stay short. For the sake of "argu-
ment" we proposed to call around for breakfast.
She scorned the idea, had "promised breakfast to
fifty already." "Staying all night? Not any." We
said we could sleep in the yard and take our chances
for breakfast. After yielding, inch by inch, she said
we could sleep on the porch. "Well, I reckon you
just as well come into the house," and showed us
into a snug room containing two nice, clean beds,
in one of which lay a little "nigger" about five years
old, with her nappy head on a snow-white pillow.
We took the floor and slept all night, and were
roused next morning to partake of a first-rate breakfast.

About eight or nine o'clock this Sunday morning we were taking our ease in and about camp,
some having gone to the river to bathe, and the
horses turned loose in the fields to graze. I was
stretched at full length on the ground, when
"bang!" went a Yankee cannon about a mile in our

rear, toward Port Republic. We were up and astir instantly, fully realizing the situation. By lending my assistance to the drivers in catching and hitching up the horses, my gun was the first ready, and started immediately in the direction of the firing, with Captain Poague in the lead, the other guns following on as they got ready.

Three or four hundred yards brought us in full view of Port Republic, situated just across the river. Beyond, and to the left of the village, was a small body of woods; below this, and lying between the river and mountain, an open plain. We fired on several regiments of infantry in the road parallel to and across the river, who soon began moving off to the left. The other guns of the battery, arriving on the scene one at a time, took position on our left and opened vigorously on the retreating infantry. My gun then moved forward and unlimbered close to a bridge about two hundred yards below the town, where we took position on a bluff in the bend of the river. We commenced firing at the enemy's cavalry as they emerged from the woods and crossed the open plain. One of our solid shots struck a horse and rider going at full gallop. The horse reared straight up, then down both fell in a common heap to rise no more.

While in this position General Jackson, who had narrowly escaped being captured in his quarters in the town, came riding up to us. Soon after his arrival we saw a single piece of artillery pass by the lower end of the village, and, turning to the right, drive quietly along the road toward the bridge. The men were dressed in blue, most of them having on blue overcoats; still we were confident they were our own men, as three-fourths of us wore captured overcoats. General Jackson ordered, "Fire on that gun!" We said, "General, those are our men." The General repeated, "Fire on that gun!" Captain Poague said, "General, I know those are our men." (Poague has since told me that he had, that morning, crossed the river and seen one of our batteries in camp near this place.) Then the General called, "Bring that gun over here," and repeated the order several times. We had seen, a short distance behind us, a regiment of our infantry, the Thirty-seventh Virginia. It was now marching in column very slowly toward us. In response to Jackson's order to "bring that gun over here," the Federals, for Federals they were, unlimbered their gun and pointed it through the bridge. We tried to fire, but could not depress our gun sufficiently for a good aim.

The front of the infantry regiment had now reached a point within twenty steps of us on our right, when the Federals turned their gun toward us and fired, killing the five men of the regiment at the front. The Federals then mounted their horses and limber, leaving their gun behind, and started off. The infantry, shocked by their warm reception, had not yet recovered. We called on them, over and over, to kill a horse as the enemy drove off. They soon began shooting, and, I thought, fired shots enough to kill a dozen horses; but on the Federals went, right in front of us, and not more than one hundred yards distant, accompanied by two officers on horseback. When near the town the horse of one officer received a shot and fell dead. The Thirty-seventh Virginia followed on in column through the bridge, its front having passed the deserted gun while its rear was passing us. The men in the rear, mistaking the front of their own regiment for the enemy, opened fire on them, heedless of the shouts of their officers and of the artillerymen as to what they were doing. I saw a little fellow stoop, and, resting his rifle on his knee, take a long aim and fire. Fortunately, they shot no better at their own men than they did at the enemy, as not a man was touched. Up to this time we had been absorbed in events immediately at hand, but, quiet being now restored, we heard cannonading back toward Harrisonburg. Fremont had attacked Ewell at Cross Keys about four miles from us. Soon the musketry was heard and the battle waxed warm.

Remaining in this position the greater portion of the day, we listened anxiously to learn from the increasing or lessening sound how the battle was going with Ewell, and turned our eyes constantly in the opposite direction, expecting a renewal of the attack from Shields. Toward the middle of the afternoon the sound became more and more remote

—Ewell had evidently been victorious, which fact was later confirmed by couriers. We learned, too, of the death of General Ashby, which had occurred the preceding day, and that his body had been borne through our camp just before the alarm of that morning. In an encounter with the First New Jersey Cavalry, which was led by Colonel Percy Windham, an Englishman who was captured in the mêlée, Ashby's horse was killed under him; he rose, and while leading the Fifty-eighth Virginia on foot, he fell pierced by a bullet and died almost instantly.

CHAPTER VIII

BATTLE OF PORT REPUBLIC

ABOUT sundown we crossed on the bridge, and our wagons joining us we went into bivouac. In times of this kind, when every one is tired, each has to depend on himself to prepare his meal. While I was considering how best and soonest I could get my supper cooked, Bob Lee happened to stop at our fire, and said he would show me a first-rate plan. It was to mix flour and water together into a thin batter, then fry the grease out of bacon, take the meat out of the frying pan and pour the batter in, and then "just let her rip awhile over the fire." I found the receipt a good one and expeditious.

About two miles below us, near the river, we could plainly see the enemy's camp-fires. Early next morning we were astir, and crossed the other fork of the river on an improvised bridge made of boards laid on the running-gear of wagons.

We felt assured that Fremont and Shields had received ample satisfaction, and that we were done with them for the present at least. Still more were we of this opinion when the wagon-train took the Brown's Gap road leading across the Blue Ridge, we expecting, of course, to follow. We did not follow, however, but took instead the route Shields's forces had taken the day previous, along which lay the bodies of the men we had killed, their heads, with few exceptions, being shot entirely off. Having gone about a mile, the enemy opened on us with artillery, their shells tearing by us with a most venomous whistle. Halted on the sides of the road, as we moved by, were the infantry of our brigade. Among them I recognized my old school-teacher, Alfonso Smith, who had just joined the army. I had many times quailed under his fierce eye and writhed under his birch rod. The strain to which he was subjected under these circumstances was doubly trying, waiting inactive for his first baptism of fire. His eye was restless as we passed; perhaps he had a presentiment, as he received his death-wound before the day was over.

Again our two Parrott guns were ordered forward. Turning out of the road to the left, we unlimbered and commenced firing. The ground on which we stood was level and very soft, and, having no hand-spike, we had to move the trail of the gun by main force. The enemy very soon got our range, and more accurate shooting I was never subjected to. The other four guns of the battery now came up, and, passing along a small ravine about forty yards behind us, halted for a time nearby. We were hotly engaged, shells bursting close around and pelting us with soft dirt as they struck the ground. Bob Lee came creeping up from his gun in the ravine, and called to me, "Ned, that isn't making batter-cakes, is it?" The constant recoiling of our gun cut great furrows in the earth, which made it necessary to move several times to more solid ground. In these different positions which we occupied three of the enemy's shells passed between the wheels and under the axle of our gun, bursting at the trail. One of them undermined the gunner's (Henry's) footing and injured him so as to necessitate his leaving the field. Even the old Irish hero, Tom Martin, was demoralized, and, in dodging from a Yankee shell, was struck by the wheel of our gun in its recoil and rendered *hors de combat.* We had been kept in this position for two or three hours, while a flank movement was being made by Taylor's Louisiana Brigade and the Second Virginia Regiment through the brush at the foot of the mountain on our right. When it was thought that sufficient time had been allowed for them to make the detour, our whole line moved forward, the rest of the battery several hundred yards to our left. When my gun moved up an eighth of a mile nearer to the enemy, they added two guns to the three occupying the site of an old coal-hearth at the foot of the rugged mountain, so that our gun had five to contend with for an hour longer.

Graham Montgomery had become gunner in Henry's place, and proved a good one. He could not be hurried, and every time the smoke puffed from our gun their cannoneers slid right and left from the coal-hearth, then returning to their guns loaded and gave us a volley. As usual in such cases, our flanking party was longer in making their appearance than expected. The whole Federal line charged, and as they did so their ranks rapidly thinned, some hesitating to advance, while others were shot down in full view. Still they drove us back and captured one gun of our battery. Singleton, of my mess, was captured, and Lieut. Cole Davis, supposed to be mortally wounded, was left on the field. On getting back a short distance I found myself utterly exhausted, my woolen clothes wet with perspiration. Having been too tired to get out of the way when the gun fired, my eardrums kept up the vibrations for hours. Sleep soon overcame me, but still the battle reverberated in my head.

The Louisianians and the Second Virginia had gotten through the brush and driven the enemy from the field. I was roused, to join in the pursuit, and had the satisfaction of seeing the five cannon that had played on our gun standing silent on the coal-hearth, in our hands. There being no room in their rear, their caissons and limbers stood off to their right on a flat piece of heavily wooded ground. This was almost covered with dead horses. I think there must have been eighty or ninety on less than an acre; one I noticed standing almost upright, perfectly lifeless, supported by a fallen tree. Farther on we overtook one of our battery horses which we had captured from Banks two weeks before.

Shields's men then captured him from us, and we again from them. He had been wounded four times, but was still fit for service.

The other four guns of our battery were posted in a wheat-field where the faces of the men were constantly sprinkled with the milk from the half-ripe wheat, splashed by the Minies.

Such a spectacle as we here witnessed and exultingly enjoyed possibly has no parallel. After a rapid retreat of more than one hundred miles, to escape from the clutches of three armies hotly pursuing on flank and rear, one of which had outstripped us, we paused to contemplate the situation. On the ground where we stood lay the dead and wounded of Shields's army, with much of their artillery and many prisoners in our possession, while, crowning the hills in full view and with no means of crossing an intervening river, even should they venture to do so, stood another army—Fremont's—with flags flying.

The narrow road with river on one side and mountain on the other caused the closely-pressed Federals in many instances to "take to the brush." George Ailstock, of Rockbridge County, celebrated for his courage and physical strength, member of Company G, Fifty-eighth Virginia Regiment, with two or three others of his company, was in hot pursuit, following the trail of a band through broken brush and weeds, and being fleeter than his companions he outran them, and while alone overtook a party of Federals, a lieutenant and twenty-eight privates. He called on them to surrender, which they did, and when his friends came up he had formed his prisoners in line and was marching them out. When asked by the major of his regiment how he had managed to capture so many, George replied, "I just surrounded 'em, Major."

CHAPTER IX

FROM BROWN'S GAP TO STAUNTON—FROM STAUN-
TON TO RICHMOND—COLD HARBOR—GENERAL
LEE VISITS HIS SON IN THE BATTERY

I HAD exchanged my brother John as a bed-fel-
low for Walter Packard. Walter was a droll fellow, rather given to arguing, and had a way of
enraging his adversary while he kept cool, and
when it suited, could put on great dignity. Immediately following our battery, as we worked our
way along a by-road through the foothills toward
Brown's Gap, was Gen. Dick Taylor at the head of
his Louisiana Brigade. Walter had mounted and
was riding on a caisson, contrary to orders recently
issued by Jackson. Taylor ordered him to get down.
Walter turned around, and, looking coolly at him,
said, with his usual sang-froid, "Who are you, and
what the devil have you to do with my riding on a
caisson?" Taylor seemed astounded for a moment,
and then opened on poor Walter with a volley of
oaths that our champion swearer, Irish Emmett,
would have envied.

Taylor then told who he was and Walter replied,
"Excuse me, General, I have my Captain's permission to ride."

When we had gotten about half-way to the top of the mountain, I, with three others, was detailed to go back and bring Lieut. Cole Davis from the field. We were too tired for any thought but of ourselves, and retraced our steps, growling as we went. We had heard that Davis was mortally wounded, and was probably dead then. Suddenly, one hundred yards in front of us, we saw a man riding slowly toward us, sitting erect, with his plume flying. We said, "That's Davis or his ghost!" It was he, held on his horse by a man on each side. We walked on with him till dusk, but, finding he had assistants to spare, two of us overtook the battery. Davis was shot through the body, and suffering dreadfully, able to move only in an upright posture. He entirely recovered, however, and did gallant service until the close of the war.

Still photographed on my memory is the appearance of the body of one of the Second Virginia Regiment being hauled on our rear caisson. His head had been shot off, and over the headless trunk was fastened a white handkerchief, which served as a sort of guide in the darkness. Weary of plodding thus, Graham Montgomery and I left the road, a short distance from which we concluded to spend the night and be subject to no more orders. A drizzling rain was falling. Each having a gum-cloth, we spread one on the loose stones and the other over us, with our feet against a big tree, to keep from sliding down the mountain-side. We were soon asleep, and when we awoke next morning we had slid into a heap close against the tree. To give an idea of the ready access we had to the enemy's stores, I had been the possessor of nine gum-blankets within the past three weeks, and no such article as a gum-blanket was ever manufactured in the South. Any soldier carrying a Confederate canteen was at once recognized as a new recruit, as it required but a short time to secure one of superior quality from a dead foeman on a battlefield.

Following the road up the mountain, we came across one of our guns which, by bad driving, had fallen over an embankment some forty feet. Two horses still hitched to it lay on their backs, one of which I recognized as Gregory's one-eyed dun which I had ridden foraging at Bridgewater. After my arrival on top of the mountain I was sent with a detail which recovered the gun and the two horses, both alive. Dandridge and Adams were driving the team when the gun went over. They saved themselves by jumping, and came near having a fight right there as to who was at fault, and for a long time afterward it was only necessary to refer to the matter to have a repetition of the quarrel.

After a day or two we countermarched toward Port Republic and went into camp a mile from Weir's cave, where we spent several days. Thence toward Staunton and camped near the town. Here we were told that we were to have a month's rest in consideration of our long-continued marching and fighting. Rest, indeed! We lost the three days we might have had for rest while there, preparing our camp for a month of ease. During our stay here my father paid us a visit, having ridden from Lexington to see his three sons. After having gotten ourselves comfortable, orders came to pack up and be ready to move. I had carried in my knapsack a pair of lady's shoes captured from Bank's plunder at Winchester. These I gave to a camp scavenger who came from the town for plunder.

Little did we dream of the marching and fighting that were in store for us. Jackson, having vanquished three armies in the Valley, was now ordered to Richmond with his "bloody brigades."

We left Staunton about the twentieth of June, crossed the Blue Ridge at Rockfish Gap, passed through Charlottesville, and were choked, day after day, by the red dust of the Piedmont region. In Louisa County we had rain and mud to contend with, thence through the low, flat lands of Hanover, bearing to the left after passing Ashland.

Our destination was now evident. The army around Richmond was waiting for Jackson to dislodge McClellan from the Chickahominy swamps, and our attack was to be made on his right flank. It seems that our powers of endurance had been over-estimated or the distance miscalculated, as the initiatory battle at Mechanicsville was fought by A. P. Hill without Jackson's aid. This was the first of the seven days' fighting around Richmond. We arrived in the neighborhood of Cold Harbor about two P. M. on June 27, and approached more and more nearly the preliminary cannonading, most of which was done by the enemy's guns. About three o'clock the musketry began, and soon thereafter the infantry of our brigade was halted in the road alongside of us, and, loading their guns, moved forward.

In a short time the fighting became furious, done almost entirely on our side with small arms, as few positions could be found for artillery. For two or three hours the noise of the battle remained almost stationary, accentuated at intervals by the shouting of the combatants, as ground was lost or won. It was here that General Lee said to General Jackson, "That fire is very heavy! Do you think your men can stand it?" The reply was, "They can stand almost anything; they can stand that!" We stood expecting every moment to be ordered in, as every effort was made by our officers to find a piece of open ground on which we could unlimber. By sundown the firing had gradually lessened and was farther from us, and when night came on the enemy had been driven from their fortifications and quiet was restored. The loss on our side was fearful. Among the killed was my cousin, James Allen, colonel of the Second Virginia Regiment.

While lying among the guns in park that night my rest was frequently disturbed by the antics of

WILLIAM M. WILLSON
(Corporal)

one of the battery horses suffering with an attack of "blind staggers," and floundering around in the darkness among the sleeping men.

Before leaving our place of bivouac the next morning, a visit from General Lee, attended by his full staff, to his son Robert, gave us our first opportunity of seeing this grand man. The interview between father and son is described by the latter in his "Recollections and Letters of Gen. Robert E. Lee," which I quote:

"The day after the battle of Cold Harbor, during the 'Seven Days' fighting around Richmond, was the first time I met my father after I had joined General Jackson. The tremendous work Stonewall's men had performed, including the rapid march from the Valley of Virginia, the short rations, the bad water, and the great heat, had begun to tell upon us, and I was pretty well worn out. On this particular morning my battery had not moved from its bivouac ground of the previous night, but was parked in an open field, all ready waiting orders. Most of the men were lying down, many sleeping, myself among the latter number. To get some shade and to be out of the way I had crawled under a caisson, and was busy making up many lost hours of rest. Suddenly I was rudely awakened by a comrade, prodding me with a sponge-staff as I had failed to be aroused by his call, and was told to get up and come out, that some one wished to see me. Half-awake I staggered out, and found myself face

to face with General Lee and his staff.   Their fresh
uniforms, bright equipments, and well-groomed
horses contrasted so forcibly with the war-worn
appearance of our command that I was completely
dazed.   It took me a moment or two to realize what
it all meant, but when I saw my father's loving eyes
and smile it became clear to me that he had ridden
by to see if I was safe and to ask how I was getting
along.   I remember well how curiously those with
him gazed at me, and I am sure that it must have
struck them as very odd that such a dirty, ragged,
unkempt youth could have been the son of this
grand-looking victorious commander.

"I was introduced recently to a gentleman, now
living in Washington, who, when he found out my
name, said he had met me once before and that it
was on this occasion.   At that time he was a member of the Tenth Virginia Infantry, Jackson's division, and was camped near our battery.   Seeing
General Lee and staff approach, he, with others,
drew near to have a look at them, and witnessed
the meeting between father and son.   He also said
that he had often told of the incident as illustrating
the peculiar composition of our army."

As we moved on over the battlefield that morning,
the number of slain on both sides was fully in proportion to the magnitude of the conflict of the day
preceding.   In a piece of woods through which we
passed, and through which the battle had surged
back and forth, after careful observation I failed

to find a tree the size of a man's body with less than a dozen bullet-marks on it within six feet of the ground, and many of them were scarred to the tops. Not even the small saplings had escaped, yet some of the men engaged had passed through the battle untouched. I was with my messmate, William Bolling, when he here discovered and recognized the dead body of his former school-teacher, Wood McDonald, of Winchester.

On the 28th we crossed the Chickahominy on Grapevine Bridge, the long approaches to which were made of poles, thence across the York River Railroad at Savage Station. As we moved along fighting was almost constantly heard in advance of us, and rumors were rife that the trap was so set as to capture the bulk of McClellan's army. Near White Oak Swamp we reached another battlefield, and, after night, went into bivouac among the enemy's dead. About ten o'clock I, with several others, was detailed to go back with some wagons, to get a supply of captured ammunition. For four or five miles we jolted over corduroy roads, loaded our wagons, and got back to the battery just before dawn of the following morning. Scarcely had I stretched myself on the ground when the bugle sounded reveille, and even those who had spent the night undisturbed were with difficulty aroused from sleep. I remember seeing Captain Poague go to a prostrate form that did not respond to the summons, and call out, "Wake up, wake up!" But, seeing no sign of stirring, he used his foot to give it a shake, when he discovered he was trying to rouse a dead Yankee! Having been on duty all night I was being left unmolested to the last moment, when Joe Shaner came to me, as usual, and very quietly rolled up my blanket with his, to be carried on his off-horse. This was the battlefield of White Oak. Swamp, fought on June 30. Along the march from Cold Harbor we had passed several Federal field-hospitals containing their sick, some of them in tents, some lying in bunks made of poles supported on upright forks. These and their old camps were infested with vermin—"war bugs," as we usually called them—which, with what we already had after two weeks of constant march, with neither time nor material for a change, made us exceedingly uncomfortable.

CHAPTER X

GENERAL JACKSON COMPLIMENTS THE BATTERY—
MALVERN HILL—MY VISIT TO RICHMOND

ON July 1 we passed near the battlefield known
as Frazier's Farm, also fought on June 30 by the
divisions of Magruder, Longstreet, and others, and
arrived early in the day in front of Malvern Hill.
For a mile or more our road ran through a dense
body of woods extending to the high range of hills
occupied by the enemy. At a point where another
road crossed the one on which we had traveled, and
where stood two old gate-posts, we were ordered to
mount the caissons and limbers and trot on toward
the firing already begun. This order can be attributed to the reputation our battery had made, and is
a matter of record, which I quote: "At Malvern
Hill the battery was openly complimented by General Jackson in connection with Carpenter's battery.
When Gen. D. H. Hill asked General Jackson if he
could furnish him a battery which would hold a
certain position, from which two or three batteries
had been driven by the galling fire of the enemy,
he said, 'Yes, two,' and called for Carpenter and
Poague, and General Hill ordered Captain Poague
to bring up his battery at once."

Taking the road to the left, we soon emerged from the woods into a wheat-field, the grain standing in shocks. While seated on a caisson, driving down this road at a trot, I was suddenly seized with a presentiment that I was to be killed in this battle, the only time such a feeling came over me during the war. Finding myself becoming rapidly demoralized, I felt that, in order to avoid disgrace, I must get down from that seat and shake the wretched thing off. So down I jumped and took it afoot, alongside of the gun, as we passed down a little ravine which was being raked from end to end by the enemy's shells. The diversion worked like a charm, for in two minutes the apprehension toned down to the normal proportions of "stage fright." We soon were in position with our six guns ablaze. The enemy's batteries were posted on considerably higher ground, with three times as many guns and of heavier calibre than ours, which served us the same galling fire that had wrecked the batteries preceding us. After having been engaged for an hour, a battery posted some two hundred yards to our left was stampeded and came by us under whip and spur, announcing, as they passed, that they were flanked by Federal cavalry. In the commotion, some one in our battery called out that we had orders to withdraw, and, before it could be corrected, eight or ten of the company, joining in the rout, beat a retreat to the woods, for which they were afterward punished; some being assigned as drivers, and one

or two gallant fellows having it ever afterward to
dim their glory. We soon, however, recovered from
the confusion, but with diminished numbers. I
know that for a part of the time I filled the positions of 7, 5, and 2 at my gun, until a gallant little
lieutenant named Day, of some general's staff, relieved me of part of the work. My brother John,
working at the gun next to mine, received a painful
shell-wound in the side and had to leave the field.
His place was supplied by Doran, an Irishman, and
in a few minutes Doran's arm was shattered by a
shell, causing him to cry out most lustily. My
brother David, shortly after this, was disabled by
a blow on his arm, and, at my solicitation, left the
field.

I would suggest to any young man when enlist-
ing, to select a company in which he has no near
kindred. The concern as to one's own person af-
fords sufficient entertainment, without being kept
in suspense as to who went down when a shell ex-
plodes in proximity to another member of the
family.

John Fuller, driver at the piece next on my right,
was crouched down on his knees, with his head
leaning forward, holding his horses. Seeing a
large shell descending directly toward him, I called
to him to look out! When he raised his head, this
shell was within five feet of him and grazed his
back before entering the ground close behind him.
He was severely shocked, and for some days unfit

for duty. At the first battle of Fredericksburg, less than a year after this, while holding his horses and kneeling in the same posture, a shell descending in like manner struck him square on his head and passed down through the length of his body. A month after the battle I saw all that was left of his cap—the morocco vizor—lying on the ground where he was killed.

Behind us, scattered over the wheat-field, were a number of loose artillery horses from the batteries that had been knocked out. Taking advantage of the opportunity to get a meal, one of these stood eating quietly at a shock of wheat, when another horse came galloping toward him from the woods. When within about thirty yards of the animal feeding, a shell burst between the two. The approaching horse instantly wheeled, and was flying for the woods when another shell burst a few feet in front of him, turning him again to the field as before; the old warrior ate away at his shock, perfectly unconcerned.

The firing on both sides, especially on ours, was now diminishing—and soon ceased. In this encounter ten or twelve members of the company were wounded, and Frank Herndon, wheel driver at my caisson, was killed. After remaining quiet for a short time we were ordered back, and again found ourselves at the cross-roads, near the old gate-posts, which seemed to be the headquarters of Generals Lee, Jackson and D. H. Hill.

John Brown, one of our company who had been detailed to care for the wounded, had taken a seat behind a large oak-tree in the edge of the woods near us. A thirty-two-pound shot struck the tree, and, passing through the center of it, took Brown's head entirely off. We spent several hours standing in the road, which was filled with artillery, and our generals were evidently at their wits' ends. Toward evening we moved farther back into the woods, where many regiments of our infantry were in bivouac. The enemy had now turned their fire in this direction. Both that of their heavy field-pieces and gunboats, and enormous shells and solid shot, were constantly crashing through the timber, tearing off limbs and the tops of trees, which sometimes fell among the troops, maiming and killing men.

After sundown a charge was made against the enemy's left, which was repulsed with terrible loss to our men. After this the enemy continued shelling the woods; in fact their whole front, until ten o'clock at night. Our battery had moved back at least two miles and gone into park in a field, where, at short intervals, a large gunboat shell would burst over us, scattering pieces around, while the main part would whirr on, it seemed, indefinitely.

The next day, the enemy having abandoned Malvern Hill during the night, we made a rapid start in pursuit toward Harrison's Landing, but suddenly came to a halt and countermarched to a place where several roads crossed, on all of which were columns of infantry and artillery. During the remainder of the day the soldiers gave vent to their feelings by cheering the different generals as they passed to and fro, Jackson naturally receiving the lion's share.

McClellan's army being now under cover of their gunboats, and gunboats being held in mortal terror by the Confederates, we began slowly to make our way out of this loathsome place, a place which I felt should be cheerfully given up to the Northerners, where they could inhale the poisonous vapors of the bogs, and prosecute the war in continuous battle with the mosquitoes and vermin. The water of the few sluggish streams, although transparent, was highly colored by the decaying vegetable matter and the roots of the juniper. For the first time in my life I was now out of sight of the mountains. I felt utterly lost, and found myself repeatedly rising on tip-toe and gazing for a view of them in the distance. Being very much worsted physically by the campaign and malarial atmosphere, I was put on the sick-list, and given permission to go to Richmond to recuperate.

My entrance into the city contrasted strikingly with that of soldiers I had read of after a series of victories in battle. The portable forge belonging to our battery needed some repairs, which could be made at a foundry in Richmond, and, as no other conveyance was available, I took passage on it. So

I entered the city, the first I had ever visited, after dark, seated on a blacksmith-shop drawn by four mules. Not having received my eleven dollars a month for a long time, I could not pay a hotel-bill, so I climbed the fence into a wagon-yard, retired to bed in a horse-cart, and slept soundly till daylight. That morning I took breakfast with my cousin, Robert Barton, of the First Virginia Cavalry, at his boarding-house. After which, having gotten a sick furlough, he hurried to take the train, to go to his home, and left me feeling very forlorn. Thinking that I could fare no worse in camp than I would in the midst of the painful surroundings of a hospital, I returned in the afternoon to the battery. The arduous service undergone during the past three weeks, or rather three months, had left the men greatly depleted in health and vigor. Many were seriously sick, and those still on duty were more or less run-down.

CHAPTER XI

FROM RICHMOND TO GORDONSVILLE—BATTLE OF
CEDAR RUN—DEATH OF GENERAL WINDER—DE-
SERTERS SHOT—CROSS THE RAPPAHANNOCK

AT the conclusion of this sojourn in camp, Jackson's command again took the march and toiled along the line of the Central Railroad toward Gordonsville. I, being sick, was given transportation by rail in a freight-car with a mixture of troops. A week was spent in Louisa County, in the celebrated Green Spring neighborhood, where we fared well. My old mess, numbering seventeen when I joined it, had by this time been greatly reduced. My brother John had gotten a discharge from the army, his office of commissioner of chancery exempting him. He re-enlisted later and served with the battery until Appomattox. Gregory, Frank Preston and Stuart had been left in Winchester in the enemy's lines severely wounded. Singleton had been captured at Port Republic, and others were off on sick-leave. My bedfellow, Walter Packard, had contracted fever in the Chickahominy swamps, from which he soon after died. He had been left at the house of a friend in Hanover County, attended by his brother. In his delirium he impatiently rehearsed the names of his companions, calling the roll of the company over and over. From Green Spring we marched to the neighborhood of Gordonsville, where we remained in camp until about the fifth or sixth of August.

We now heard reports of the approach of the re-nowned General Pope with "headquarters in the saddle," along the line of the old Orange and Alex-andria Railroad. On August 7, we moved out of camp, going in his direction. On the third day's march, being too unwell to foot it, I was riding in the ambulance. About noon indications in front showed that a battle was at hand. I was excused from duty, but was asked by the captain if I would assist in caring for the wounded. This I declined to do. About this time the battery was ordered for-ward, and, seeing my gun start off at a trot, I mounted and rode in with it. We had a long hill to descend, from the top of which could be seen and heard the cannonading in front. Then, entering an extensive body of woods, we passed by the bod-ies of four infantrymen lying side by side, having just been killed by a bursting shell.

We took position in the road near the corner of an open field with our two Parrott guns and one gun of Carpenter's battery, en echelon, with each gun's horses and limber off on its left among the trees. Both Capt. Joe Carpenter and his brother, John, who was his first lieutenant, were with this gun, as was their custom when any one of their guns went into action. We soon let the enemy know where we were, and they replied promptly, getting our range in a few rounds.

General Winder, commander of our brigade, dismounted, and, in his shirt-sleeves, had taken his stand a few paces to the left of my gun and with his field-glass was intently observing the progress of the battle. We had been engaged less than fifteen minutes when Captain Carpenter was struck in the head by a piece of shell, from which, after lingering a few weeks, he died. Between my gun and limber, where General Winder stood, was a constant stream of shells tearing through the trees and bursting close by. While the enemy's guns were changing their position he gave some directions, which we could not hear for the surrounding noise. I, being nearest, turned and, walking toward him, asked what he had said. As he put his hand to his mouth to repeat the remark, a shell passed through his side and arm, tearing them fearfully. He fell straight back at full length, and lay quivering on the ground. He had issued strict orders that morning that no one, except those detailed for the purpose, should leave his post to carry off the wounded, in obedience to which I turned to the gun and went to work. He was soon carried off, however, and died a few hours later.

The next man struck was Major Snowden Andrews, afterward colonel of artillery. While standing near by us a shell burst as it passed him, tearing his clothes and wounding him severely. Though drawn to a stooping posture, he lived many years. Next I saw a ricocheting shell strike Captain Caskie, of Richmond, Virginia, on his seat, which knocked him eight or ten feet and his red cap some feet farther. He did not get straightened up until he had overtaken his cap on the opposite side of some bushes, through which they had both been propelled. Lieutenant Graham, of our battery, also received a painful, though not serious, wound before the day was over. This proved to be a very dangerous place for officers, but not a private soldier was touched.

By frequent firing during the campaign the vent of my gun had been burned to several times its proper size, so that at each discharge an excess of smoke gushed from it. After the captain's attention was called to it, it happened that a tree in front, but somewhat out of line, was cut off by a Federal shell just as our gun fired. Supposing the defect had caused a wild shot, we were ordered to take the gun to the rear, the other gun soon following. We got away at a fortunate time, as the Second Brigade of Jackson's division was flanked by the enemy and driven over the place a few minutes later. One company in the Twenty-first Virginia Regiment lost, in a few minutes, seventeen men killed, besides those wounded. The flankers, however, were soon attacked by fresh troops, who drove them back and took a large number of prisoners, who walked and looked, as they passed, as if they had done their

best and had nothing of which to be ashamed.   By nightfall the whole of Pope's army had been driven back, and we held the entire battlefield.   This battle was called Cedar Run by the Confederates, and Slaughter's Mountain by the Federals.

On the following day we retraced our steps and occupied an excellent camping-ground near Gordonsville.   Shortly after our arrival, my brother David, who had been absent on sick-leave, returned from home, bringing a large mess-chest of delicious edibles, which we enjoyed immensely, having Willie Preston, from Lexington, who had just joined the College company, to dine with us.   From a nearby cornfield we managed to supply ourselves with roasting ears, and the number a young Confederate could consume in a day would have been ample rations for a horse.

While here we had visits from some of our former messmates.   One of them, Frank Singleton, after being captured at Port Republic had been taken to Fort Warren, where were in confinement as prisoners members of the Maryland legislature, Generals Pillow and Buckner, and others captured at Fort Donelson.   Singleton gave glowing accounts of the "to-do" that was made over him, he being the only representative from the army of Stonewall, whose fame was now filling the world.   His presence even became known outside of prison-walls, and brought substantial tokens of esteem and sympathy.

Robert A. Gibson

Gregory, who we supposed had received his death-wound at Winchester in May, after escaping into our lines spent a day or two with us. Both, however, having gotten discharges, left us—Singleton to go to Kentucky, his native State, to raise a company of cavalry under Morgan, and Gregory to become captain of ordnance.

An extensive move was evidently now on foot, and about August 17th it began, proving to be by far the most eventful of that eventful year. On reaching the Rapidan, a few miles distant, we were ordered to leave all baggage we could not carry on our backs, and in that August weather we chose to make our burdens light. This was the last we saw of our baggage, as it was plundered and stolen by camp-followers and shirkers who stayed behind.

Having recuperated somewhat during my stay in camp I had set out, with the battery, for the march, but a few days of hot sun soon weakened me again, so I had to be excused from duty, and remain with the wagons. Part of a day with them was sufficient, so I returned to the battery, sick or well. Soon after my return, about sundown, Arthur Robinson, of Baltimore, whom I had regarded as a sort of dude, brought me a cup of delicious tea and several lumps of cut loaf-sugar. Cut loaf-sugar! What associations it awakened and how kindly I felt toward the donor ever afterward! As I dropped each lump into the tea I could sympathize with an old lady in Rockbridge County, who eyed a lump of it lovingly and said, "Before the war I used to buy that *by the pound.*"

On the following morning, August 18, Gen. J. E. B. Stuart came dashing into our camp bareheaded and, for him, very much excited. He had just narrowly escaped capture by a scouting-party of Federal cavalry at a house near Verdiersville, where he had passed the night. Leaving his hat, he mounted and leaped the fence with his horse. His adjutant, however, Major Fitzhugh, in possession of General Lee's instructions to General Stuart, was captured, and thus General Pope informed of the plan of campaign. Four days later General Stuart, with a large force of cavalry, having passed to the rear of the Federal army, captured, at Catlett's Station, General Pope's headquarters wagon with his official papers and personal effects. As his plan of campaign was to be governed by General Lee's movements, these papers were not very reliable guides.

Our stay in this bivouac was only thirty-six hours in duration, but another scene witnessed in the afternoon leaves an indelible impression. To escape the arduous service to which we had for some time been subjected, a few, probably eight or ten men, of Jackson's old division had deserted. Of these, three had been caught, one of whom was a member of the Stonewall Brigade, and they were sentenced by court-martial to be shot. As a warning to others, the whole division was mustered out to witness the painfully solemn spectacle. After marching in column through intervening woods, with bands playing the dead march, we entered an extensive field. Here the three men, blindfolded, were directed to kneel in front of their open graves, and a platoon of twelve or fifteen men, half of them with their muskets loaded with ball, and half with blank cartridges (so that no man would feel that he had fired a fatal shot), at the word "Fire!" emptied their guns at close range. Then the whole division marched by within a few steps to view their lifeless bodies.

Jackson's object now was to cross the Rappahannock, trying first one ford and then another. We spent most of the following day galloping to and fro, firing and being fired at. At one ford my gun crossed the river, but, as no support followed it, although the rest of our battery and Brockenbrough's Maryland Battery were close by, we soon recrossed. Rain during the afternoon and night made the river past fording, catching Early's brigade, which had crossed further up-stream, on the enemy's side. He was not pressed, however, and by the next afternoon the whole of Jackson's command had crossed the stream by the fords nearer its source, at Hinson's mill. Thence we traveled northwest through Little Washington, the county-seat of Rappahannock. Then to Flint Hall, at the base of the Blue Ridge. Then turned southeast into Fauquier County and through Warrenton, the prettiest town

I had seen since leaving the Valley. We had made an extensive detour, and were no longer disturbed by General Pope, who possibly thought Jackson was on his way to Ohio or New York, and a week later no doubt regretted that one of those distant places had not been his destination.

Before reaching Thoroughfare Gap we had the pleasure of a visit from Mr. Robert Bolling, or rather found him waiting on the roadside to see his son, of our mess, having driven from his home in the neighborhood. His son had been left behind sick, but his messmates did full justice to the bountiful supply of refreshments brought in the carriage for him. I remember, as we stood regaling ourselves, when some hungry infantryman would fall out of ranks, and ask to purchase a "wee bite," how delicately we would endeavor to "shoo" him off, without appearing to the old gentleman as the natural heirs to what he had brought for his boy.

CHAPTER XII

OUR halts and opportunities for rest had been
and continued to be few and of short duration, traveling steadily on throughout the twenty-four hours.
It has been many years since, but how vividly some
scenes are recalled, others vague and the order of
succession forgotten. After passing through Thoroughfare Gap we moved on toward Manassas Junction, arriving within a mile or two of the place
shortly after dawn, when we came upon a sleepy
Federal cavalryman mounted on a fine young horse.
Lieutenant Brown took him and his arms in charge
and rode the horse for a few days, but, learning that
he had been taken from a farmer in the neighborhood, returned him to his owner. As we approached
the Junction several cannon-shots warned us that
some force of the enemy was there, but not General Pope, as we had left him many miles in our
rear.

In the regiment of our cavalry, acting as a vanguard, I had but two acquaintances—old college-
mates—and these were the only two members of the

command I met. One of them gave me a loaf of baker's bread, the other presented me with a handful of cigars, and they both informed us that they had made a big capture, which we would soon see. The samples they had brought made us the more anxious. Arriving in sight of the place, we saw the tracks of both railroads closely covered for half a mile with the cars filled with army supplies of every description. The artillery that had been firing a short time before opened on us again, while we were preparing to help ourselves, but not before one of my messmates had secured a cup of molasses. With the help of this, my loaf of bread was soon devoured and with a relish contrasting very favorably with my sudden loss of appetite for the beans at Cedar Creek a few months before. On this occasion we managed to appease our hunger with very little interruption from the flying shells. The firing, however, was at long range and soon ceased, and we resumed the march, saddened to part with so rich a booty and the opportunity to fill our stomachs and empty haversacks.

As we moved quietly along with General Jackson and one or two of his staff riding at the front of the battery, there suddenly appeared, about a mile ahead of us, a line of bayonets glistening in the sunlight. As we halted I heard General Jackson and those about him questioning each other and speculating as to what troops they could be, whether friend or foe. Their bayonets were evidently too bright for our war worn weapons, and the direction from which they came and, a little later, the color of their uniforms being distinguishable, no longer left room for doubt. It proved to be a brigade of New Jersey infantry commanded by General Taylor, who had just arrived by rail from Alexandria. Rodes's division was on our left and not three hundred yards distant. As the enemy advanced, Jackson ordered Rodes to halt. The Federal brigade came up on our right about one hundred and twenty-five yards from us, marching by companies in column.

Jackson ordered us to fire on them with canister, which we did, and very rapidly, as they passed. Then, limbering up, we galloped again to their flank and repeated the operation; meanwhile, one of our batteries immediately in their front firing at them with shells. Jackson, who accompanied us, then drew a white handkerchief from his pocket, and, waving it up and down, ordered them to surrender, in response to which one of them raised his gun and fired deliberately at him. I heard the Minie as it whistled by him. After limbering up our guns for the third time to keep in close range, I turned to get my blanket, which I had left on the ground while engaged, and, as I ran to overtake the guns, found myself between Rodes's line, which had now advanced, and the Federals, in easy range of each other. I expected, of course, to be riddled with bullets, but neither side fired a shot.

The Federals moved on in perfect order, then suddenly broke and came back like a flock of sheep; and, most singular of all, Rodes's division was ordered back and let them pass, we still firing. It was a fine sample of a sham battle, as I saw none of them killed and heard there were very few casualties, and the only shot they fired was the one at General Jackson. After crossing a ravine along which ran a creek, they had a hill to ascend which kept them still in full view, while we fired at them with shells and solid shot as they streamed along the paths. Maupin, a member of our detachment, picked up a canteen of whiskey which had been thrown aside in their flight. As it was the only liquid to which we had access on that hot August day, we each took a turn, and soon undertook to criticise our gunner's bad shooting, telling him among other things that if he would aim lower he would do more execution.

After the enemy had disappeared from our sight, and the battery had gone into park, I borrowed Sergeant Dick Payne's horse to ride to the creek, over which the enemy had retreated, for a canteen of water. When within a few steps of the branch, I passed two artillerymen from another battery on foot, who were on the same errand, but none of us armed. We saw a Yankee infantryman a short distance off, hurrying along with gun on shoulder. We called to him to surrender, and, as I rode to get his gun, another one following came in sight. When

I confronted him and ordered him to throw down
his gun, he promptly obeyed. The gun, a brand-
new one, was loaded, showing a bright cap under
the hammer. The man was a German, and tried
hard, in broken English, to explain, either how he
had fallen behind, or to apologize for coming to
fight us—I could not tell which.

We now had full and undisturbed possession of
Manassas Junction and of the long trains of captured cars, through the doors and openings of which
could be seen the United States army supplies of all
kinds and of the best quality. On a flat car there
stood two new pieces of artillery made of a bronze-
colored metal, and of a different style from any we
had yet seen. In our last battle, that of Slaughter's
Mountain, we had noticed, for the first time, a singular noise made by some of the shells fired at us,
and quite like the shrill note of a tree-frog on a big
scale. Since then we had sometimes speculated as
to what new engine of war we had to contend with.
Here it was, and known as the three-inch rifled gun,
a most accurate shooter, and later on much used by
both Federals and Confederates.

In view of the fact that almost all of the field
artillery used by the Confederates was manufactured in the North, a supply for both armies seemed
to have been wisely provided in the number they
turned out. Here we spent the remainder of the
day, but not being allowed to plunder the cars did
not have the satisfaction of replacing our worn-out

garments with the new ones in sight. We were very willing to don the blue uniforms, but General Jackson thought otherwise. What we got to eat was also disappointing, and not of a kind to invigorate, consisting, as it did, of hard-tack, pickled oysters, and canned stuff generally.

Darkness had scarcely fallen before we were again on the march, and before two miles had been traveled the surrounding country was illuminated by the blazing cars and their contents, fired to prevent their falling again into the hands of their original owners. The entire night was spent marching through woods and fields, but in what direction we had no idea. Notwithstanding the strict orders to the contrary, two of our boys—Billy Bumpas and John Gibbs—had procured from a car about half a bushel of nice white sugar, put it in a sack-bag, and tied it securely, they thought, to the axle of a caisson. During the night either the bag stretched or the string slipped, letting a corner drag on the ground, which soon wore a hole. When daylight broke, the first thing that met their eager gaze was an empty bag dangling in the breeze and visions of a trail of white sugar mingling with the dust miles behind. Many times afterward, in winter quarters or during apple-dumpling season, have I heard them lament the loss of that sweetening.

There are various scenes and incidents on the battlefield, in camp, and on the march which leave an indelible impression. Of these, among the most

D. Gardiner Tyler

vivid to me is that of a column of men and horses at dawn of day, after having marched throughout the night. The weary animals, with heads hanging and gaunt sides, put their feet to the ground as softly as if fearing to arouse their drowsy mates or give themselves a jar. A man looks some years older than on the preceding day, and his haggard face as if it had been unwashed for a week. Not yet accustomed to the light, and thinking his countenance unobserved, as in the darkness, he makes no effort to assume an expression more cheerful than in keeping with his solemn feelings, and, when spoken to, his distressful attempt to smile serves only to emphasize the need of "sore labor's bath." Vanity, however, seems to prevent each one from seeing in his neighbor's visage a photograph of his own. But, with an hour of sunlight and a halt for breakfast with a draught of rare coffee, he stands a new creature. On the morning after our departure from Manassas Junction, having marched all night, we had a good illustration of this.

About seven o'clock we came to a Federal wagon which had upset over a bank and was lying, bottom upward, in a ditch below the road. Around it were boxes and packages of food, desiccated vegetables red with tomatoes and yellow with pumpkin. Here a timely halt was called. Across the ditch, near where we went into park, the infantry who had preceded us had carried from the overturned wagon a barrel of molasses with the head knocked out. Surging around it was a swarm of men with canteens, tin cups, and frying-pans—anything that would hold molasses. As each vessel was filled by a dip into the barrel it was held aloft, to prevent its being knocked from the owner's grasp as he made his way out through the struggling mass; and woe be to him that was hatless! as the stream that trickled from above, over head and clothes, left him in a sorry plight.

CHAPTER XIII

CIRCUITOUS NIGHT MARCH—FIRST DAY OF SECOND
MANASSAS—ARRIVAL OF LONGSTREET'S CORPS

HERE we halted long enough for a hurried breakfast for men and horses. Sleep did not seem to enter
into Jackson's calculations, or time was regarded as
too precious to be allowed for it. We were on the
move again by noon and approaching the scene of
the battle of July, 1861. This was on Thursday,
August 26, 1862, and a battle was evidently to open
at any moment. In the absence of Henry, our gunner, who was sick and off duty, I was appointed to
fill his place. And it was one of the few occasions,
most probably the only one during the war, that I
felt the slightest real desire to exclaim, with the Corporal at Waterloo, "Let the battle begin!" About
two P. M. we went into position, but, before firing
a shot, suddenly moved off, and, marching almost in
a semi-circle, came up in the rear of the infantry,
who were now hotly engaged. This was the beginning of the second battle of Manassas, during the
first two days of which, and the day preceding,
Jackson's command was in great suspense, and,
with a wide-awake and active foe, would have been
in great jeopardy. He was entirely in the rear of

the Federal army, with only his own corps, while
Longstreet had not yet passed through Thoroughfare Gap, a narrow defile miles away. The rapid
and steady roll of the musketry, however, indicated
that there was no lack of confidence on the part of
his men, though the line of battle had changed front
and was now facing in the opposite direction from
the one held a few hours before. Moving through
a body of woods toward the firing-line we soon began meeting and passing the stream of wounded
men making their way to the rear. And here our
attention was again called to a singular and unac-
countable fact, which was noticed and remarked repeatedly throughout the war. It was that in one
battle the large majority of the less serious wounds
received were in the same portion of the body. In
this case, fully three-fourths of the men we met
were wounded in the left hand; in another battle
the same proportion were wounded in the right
hand; while in another the head was the attractive
mark for flying bullets, and so on. I venture the
assertion that every old soldier whose attention is
called to it will verify the statement.

The battle was of about two hours duration, and
by sundown the firing had entirely ceased, the enemy
being driven from the field, leaving their dead and
wounded. The infantry of the Stonewall Brigade
had been in the thickest of it all and had suffered
severe loss.

Willie Preston, of the College company, less than

eighteen years of age, a most attractive and promising youth, received a mortal wound. His dying messages were committed to Hugh White, the captain of his company, who, two days later, was himself instantly killed. On the ground where some of the heaviest fighting took place there stood a neat log house, the home of a farmer's family. From it they had, of course, hurriedly fled, leaving their cow and a half-grown colt in the yard. Both of these were killed. I saw also, on this field, a dead rabbit and a dead field-lark—innocent victims of man's brutality!

A quiet night followed, and, except for those of us who were on guard, the first unbroken rest we had had for almost a week. Next morning, after breakfasting leisurely, we went into position opposite the enemy, who occupied a long range of hills too distant for serious damage. But, after we had shelled each other for half an hour, one of our infantry regiments emerged from the woods a short distance to our right and stood in line of battle most needlessly exposed. In less than five minutes a shell burst among them, killing and wounding eleven men. This over, we moved to a haystack nearby, where our horses had more than one refreshing feed during lulls in the battle. It seemed, also, an attractive place for General Jackson, as he was seldom far from it till the close of the battle on the following day.

An hour later, while engaged in another artillery

encounter, our detachment received a very peremptory and officious order from Major Shoemaker, commanding the artillery of the division. My friend and former messmate, W. G. Williamson, now a lieutenant of engineers, having no duty in that line to perform, had hunted us up, and, with his innate gallantry, was serving as a cannoneer at the gun. Offended at Shoemaker's insolent and ostentatious manner, we answered him as he deserved. Furious at such impudence and insubordination, he was almost ready to lop our heads off with his drawn sword, when Williamson informed him that he was a commissioned officer and would see him at the devil before he would submit to such uncalled-for interference.

"If you are a commissioned officer," Shoemaker replied, "why are you here, working at a gun?"

"Because I had not been assigned to other duty," was Williamson's reply, "and I chose to come back, for the time being, with my old battery."

"Then I order you under arrest for your disrespect to a superior officer!" said Shoemaker.

The case was promptly reported to General Jackson, and Williamson as promptly released. The bombastic major had little idea that among the men he was so uselessly reprimanding was a son of General Lee, as well as Lieutenant Williamson, who was a nephew of Gen. Dick Garnett, who was later killed in Pickett's charge at Gettysburg. This episode over, we again drove to the haystack.

These repeated advances and attacks made by
the enemy's artillery plainly showed that they realized that our situation was a hazardous one, of
which we, too, were fully aware, and unless Longstreet should soon show up we felt that the whole
of Pope's army would be upon us. While quietly
awaiting developments, we heard the sound of a
horse's hoofs, and, as a courier galloped up to General Jackson, to announce Longstreet's approach,
the cloud of red dust raised by his vanguard in the
direction of Thoroughfare Gap assured us that he
would soon be at hand. Before he reached the field,
however, and while we were enjoying the sense of
relief at his coming, one of the enemy's batteries
had quietly and unobserved managed to get into
one of the positions occupied by our battery during
the morning. Their first volley, coming from such
an unexpected quarter, created a great commotion.
Instantly we galloped to their front and unlimbered
our guns at close range. Other of our batteries
fired a few shots, but soon ceased, all seeming intent on witnessing a duel between the two batteries
of four guns each. Their position was the more
favorable, as their limbers and caissons were behind
the crest of the hill, while we were on level ground
with ours fully exposed. Each man worked as if
success depended on his individual exertions, while
Captain Poague and Lieutenant Graham galloped
back and forth among the guns, urging us to our
best efforts. Our antagonists got our range at once,

and, with their twelve-pound Napoleon guns, poured in a raking fire. One shell I noticed particularly as it burst, and waited a moment to observe its effects as the fragments tore by. One of them struck Captain Poague's horse near the middle of the hip, tearing an ugly hole, from which there spurted a stream of blood the size of a man's wrist. To dismount before his horse fell required quick work, but the captain was equal to the occasion. Another shell robbed Henry Boteler of the seat of his trousers, but caused the shedding of no blood, and his narrow escape the shedding of no tears, although the loss was a serious one. Eugene Alexander, of Moorefield, had his thigh-bone broken and was incapacitated for service. Sergeant Henry Payne, a splendid man and an accomplished scholar, was struck by a solid shot just below the knee and his leg left hanging by shreds of flesh. An hour later, when being lifted into an ambulance, I heard him ask if his leg could not be saved, but in another hour he was dead.

After an hour of spirited work, our antagonists limbered up and hurried off, leaving us victors in the contest. Lieutenant Baxter McCorkle galloped over to the place to see what execution we had done, and found several dead men, as many or more dead horses, and one of their caissons as evidences of good aim; and brought back with him a fine army-pistol left in the caisson. When the affair was over, I found myself exhausted and faint from overexertion in the hot sun. Remembering that my brother David had brought along a canteen of vinegar, gotten in the big capture of stores a few days before, and thinking a swallow of it would revive me, I went to him and asked him to get it for me. Before I was done speaking, the world seemed to make a sudden revolution and turn black as I collapsed with it. My brother, thinking I was shot, hurried for the vinegar, but found the canteen, which hung at the rear of a caisson, entirely empty; it, too, having been struck by a piece of shell, and even the contents of the little canteen demanded by this insatiable plain, whose thirst no amount of blood seemed able to quench.

CHAPTER XIV

THE SECOND BATTLE OF MANASSAS—INCIDENTS AND SCENES ON THE BATTLEFIELD

THESE encounters were the preludes to the great battle for which both sides were preparing, almost two days having already been spent in maneuvering and feeling each other's lines. The afternoon, however, passed quietly with no further collisions worthy of mention. The following day, Saturday, was full of excitement. It was the third and last of this protracted battle, and the last for many a brave soldier in both armies.

The shifting of troops began early, our battery changing position several times during the forenoon. Neither army had buried its dead of the first day's battle. We held the ground on which were strewn the corpses of both Blue and Gray, in some places lying side by side. The hot August sun had parched the grass to a crisp, and it was frequently ignited by bursting shells. In this way the clothes of the dead were sometimes burned off, and the bodies partially roasted! Such spectacles made little or no impression at the time, and we moved to and fro over the field, scarcely heeding them.

About two o'clock we were ordered some distance forward, to fire on a battery posted on a low ridge

near a piece of woods.   By skirting along a body of
woods on our left, and screened by it, we came out
in full view of this battery and on its right flank.
My gun, being in front and the first seen by them,
attracted their whole fire; but most of their shells
passed over our heads and burst among the guns in
our rear and among the trees.   None of us was hurt,
and in a few minutes all four of our guns were unlimbered and opened on them most vigorously.   In
five or six rounds their guns ceased firing and were
drawn by hand from the crest of the ridge entirely
out of view and range.

As we stood by our guns, highly gratified with
our prowess, General Jackson came riding up to the
first detachment and said, "That was handsomely
done, very handsomely done," then passed on to the
other detachments and to each one addressed some
complimentary remark.   In half an hour we were
again at our rendezvous, the haystack, and he at his
headquarters, and all quiet.   But this time it was
the calm before the real storm.

Across the open plains on which we stood, and
some three hundred yards distant from us, was an
extensive body of woods in which Longstreet's corps
had quietly formed in line of battle.   In front of
this was open ground, sloping gently for one-fourth
of a mile, and on its crest the enemy's line of battle.
To our left another large body of woods extended
toward our front, and concealed the movements of
both armies from view in that direction.   General

Jackson had dismounted from his horse and was sitting on the rail-fence, and ours and one or two other batteries were in bivouac close by, and all as calm and peaceful as if the armies were in their respective winter quarters, when a roar and crash of musketry that was almost deafening burst forth in the woods in our immediate front, and a shower of Minie-bullets whistled through the air, striking here and there about us. Instantly everything was astir, with an occasional lamentation or cry of pain from some wounded man. General Jackson mounted his horse hurriedly. The fighting soon became general throughout the lines, in portions of it terrific. General Pope, after two days of preparation, had advanced his lines and made the attack instead of receiving it, as our lines were on the eve of advancing.

A projected but uncompleted railroad, with alternating cuts and embankments, afforded a splendid line of defense to our infantry on the left. The most continued and persistent fighting was where it began, on that portion of the line held by Jackson's old division. In the course of an hour the attack was repulsed and a counter-charge made, but, judging from the number of dead the enemy left on the field, and the rapidity of their pursuit, the Confederates met with but little resistance thereafter. An attack had been made on Longstreets's corps at the same time, which met with the same ill success, and was followed by a countercharge. I remember our noticing the high range of hills in front of Longstreet, completely commanding, as it did, the intervening ground, and some one remarking, while the charge was in progress, that it seemed impossible to carry it. But the reserves who occupied this high ground made but little resistance, and, joining those who had been repulsed, all fled hurriedly from the field. As soon as the retreat of the Federal army began, active participation in the battle by the artillery ceased. We joined in the pursuit, which was brought to a close soon after it began by approaching night.

In crossing a field in the pursuit, a short distance from our gun, I passed near a young infantryman lying entirely alone, with his thigh-bone broken by a Minie-bullet. He was in great distress of mind and body, and asked me most pleadingly to render him some assistance. If I could do nothing else, he begged that I should find his brother, who belonged to Johnston's battery, of Bedford County, Virginia. I told him I could not leave my gun, etc., which gave him little comfort; but he told me his name, which was Ferguson, and where his home was. Fortunately, however, I happened on Johnston's battery soon after, and sent his brother to him. I heard nothing further of him until five years later—two years after the war—when I was on a visit to some relatives in Bedford County. As we started to church in Liberty one Sunday morning I recalled the incident and mentioned it to my aunt's family, and was informed that Ferguson was still alive, had been very recently married, and that I would probably see him that morning at church. And sure enough, I was scarcely seated in church when he camp limping in and took a seat near me. I recognized him at once, but, fearing he had not forgotten what he felt was cruel indifference in his desperate situation, did not renew our acquaintance.

After parting with him on the battlefield and overtaking my gun, our route for a time was through the enemy's dead and wounded of the battle which took place two days before, who had been lying between the two armies, exposed to the hot sun since that time. While taking a more direct route, as the battery was winding around an ascent, my attention was called to a Federal soldier of enormous size lying on the ground. His head was almost as large as a half-bushel and his face a dark-blue color. I supposed, as a matter of course, that he was dead, and considered him a curiosity even as a dead man. But, while standing near him, wondering at the size of the monster, he began to move, and turned as if about to rise to his feet. Thinking he might succeed, I hurried on and joined my gun.

Here we had a good opportunity of observing the marked and striking difference between the Federals and Confederates who remained unburied for twenty-four hours or more after being killed. While the Confederates underwent no perceptible change in color or otherwise, the Federals, on the contrary, became much swollen and discolored. This was, of course, attributable to the difference in their food and drink. And while some Confederates, no doubt for want of sufficient food, fell by the wayside on the march, the great majority of them, owing to their simple fare, could endure, and unquestionably did endure, more hardship than the Federals who were overfed and accustomed to regular and full rations.

Our following in the pursuit was a mere form, as the enemy had been driven by our infantry from all of their formidable positions, and night, as usual in such cases, had put a stop to further pursuit. As we countermarched, to find a suitable camping-ground, great care had to be taken in the darkness to avoid driving over the enemy's wounded who lay along the course of our route. I remember one of them especially, in a narrow place, was very grateful to me for standing near him and cautioning the drivers as they passed by.

On the next day, Sunday, August 31, after three days of occupation such as I have described, we were not averse to a Sabbath-day's rest, which also gave us the opportunity of reviewing at leisure the events and results of our experience, and going over other portions of the battlefield. Looking to the right front, spread out in full view, was the sloping ground over which Longstreet had fought and driven his antagonists. The extensive area presented the appearance of an immense flower-garden, the prevailing blue thickly dotted with red, the color of the Federal Zouave uniform. In front of the railroad-cut, and not more than fifty yards from it, where Jackson's old division had been attacked, at least three-fourths of the men who made the charge had been killed, and lay in line as they had fallen. I looked over and examined the ground carefully, and was confident that I could have walked a quarter of a mile in almost a straight line on their dead bodies without putting a foot on the ground. By such evidences as this, our minds had been entirely disabused of the idea that "the Northerners would not fight."

It was near this scene of carnage that I also saw two hundred or more citizens whose credulity under General Pope's assurance had brought them from Washington and other cities to see "Jackson bagged," and enjoy a gala day. They were now under guard, as prisoners, and responded promptly to the authority of those who marched them by at a lively pace. This sample of gentlemen of leisure gave an idea of the material the North had in reserve, to be utilized, if need be, in future.

During the three days—28th, 29th and 30th— the official reports give the Federal losses as 20,000, the Confederates as 10,000. On each of these days our town of Lexington had lost one of her most promising young men—Henry R. Payne, of our battery; Hugh White, captain of the College company, and Willie Preston, a private in the same company, a noble young fellow who had had the fortitude and moral courage, at the request of President

Junkin, to pull down the palmetto flag hoisted by the students over Washington College. We remained about Manassas only long enough for the dead to be buried.

The suffering of the wounded for want of attention, bad enough at best, in this case must have been extraordinary. The aggregate of wounded of the two armies, Confederate and Federal, exceeded 15,000 in number. The surrounding country had been devastated by war until it was practically a desert. The railroad bridges and tracks, extending from the Rapidan in Orange County to Fairfax, a distance of fifty miles, had been destroyed, so that it would require several weeks before the Confederates could reach the hospitals in Richmond and Charlottesville, and then in box-cars, over rough, improvised roads. Those of the Federal army were cut off in like manner from their hospitals in the North. In addition to all this, the surgeons and ambulances and their corps continued with their respective commands, to meet emergencies of like nature, to be repeated before the September moon had begun to wane.

CHAPTER XV

AFTER such prolonged marching and such a victory as the second Manassas we hoped for a rest so well earned; at any rate, we imagined that there was no enemy near inclined to give battle; but on Monday, September 1, we were again on the march, which continued far into the night, it being near daylight when we went into park. The latter part of the way I rode on a caisson, seated by a companion, and so entirely overcome with sleep as to be unable to keep my eyes open five seconds at a time, nodding from side to side over the wheels. My companion would rouse me and tell me of my danger, but shame, danger, and all were of no avail till, waking for the fortieth time, I found my hat was gone. I jumped down, went back a short distance, and found my old drab fur, of Lexington make, flat in the road, having been trampled over by several teams and gun-wheels.

After a halt of a few hours we were again on the move, and soon found ourselves in Fairfax County. About noon we passed by "Chantilly," the home of my messmate, Wash. Stuart, whom we had left desperately wounded at Winchester. The place, a beautiful country residence, was deserted now. Stuart, though, was somewhere in the neighborhood, a paroled prisoner, and on his return to us the following winter told us of the efforts he had made to find us near "The Plains" with a feast of wines, etc., for our refreshment. Two or three miles from Chantilly short and frequent halts and cautious advances warned us that there were breakers ahead. Then the pop, pop, pop! of a skirmish-line along the edge of a wood in our front brought back again those nervous pulsations in the region of the stomach which no amount of philosophy or will-power seemed able to repress.

The battery kept straight on in the road and through the woods, the enemy's skirmishers having fallen back to our right. We halted where the road began to descend, waiting until a place suitable for action could be found. Up to this time there was only infantry skirmishing, not a cannon having been fired on either side, when, as we stood quietly by our guns, a Federal shell burst in our midst with a tremendous crash. None of us heard the report of the gun that sent it, or knew from what direction it came, but the accuracy with which we had been located in the dense forest was not comforting.

Soon after this, our attention was attracted by the approach, along the road in our front, of ten or twelve horsemen, riding leisurely toward us, one of whom bore a banner of unusually large size. As they passed, the most conspicuous figure in the party was a Federal officer clad in brilliant uniform and mounted on a superb bay horse, who with several other prisoners was being escorted by a squad of cavalry. The banner was the flag of New York State, with the field of white-satin emblazoned with the coat-of-arms of the Empire State and all elaborately decorated with flowing cords and tassels. The officer I afterwards learned had been at West Point with Gen. Fitz Lee, and asked that his beautiful animal be given to this former friend—and the horse became the mount of Lieut. John Lee, a brother of the General.

After remaining here for an hour, and our officers finding no open ground for battle, and no enemy in sight except some videttes who saluted us with an occasional Minie-ball, we countermarched one-half mile in a drenching rain and went into park. Meanwhile, a brisk musketry fire had extended along the infantry lines, and soon after halting two of our battery horses fell dead, struck by their stray bullets. It was during this contest, in the pouring rain, that General Jackson, on receiving a message from a brigadier that his ammunition was wet, and he feared he could not hold on, replied, "Tell him to hold his ground. If his guns will not go off, neither will the enemy's."

Before the firing ceased, which continued through the twilight, Major-General Kearney, mistaking a line of Confederates for his own men, rode almost into their midst before discovering his error. He

wheeled his horse, and, as he dashed off, leaning forward on the horse's neck, received a bullet in his
back and fell dead upon the field.   Next day his
body was returned to his friends under flag of truce.

From Chantilly, or Ox Hill, as this battle was
called by Confederates and Federals, respectively,
we reached Leesburg, the county-seat, by a march of
thirty miles due north into Loudoun County, and a
mile or two east of this attractive town went into
bivouac about sunset in a beautiful grassy meadow
which afforded what seemed to us a downy couch,
and to the horses luxuriant pasturage, recalling
former and better days.   Next morning, while lying
sound asleep wrapped in my blanket, I became painfully conscious of a crushing weight on my foot.
Opening my eyes, there stood a horse almost over
me, quietly cropping the grass, with one forefoot
planted on one of mine. Having no weapon at hand,
I motioned and yelled at him most lustily.   Being
the last foot put down it was the last taken up, and,
turning completely around, he twisted the blanket
around the calks of his shoe, stripped it entirely off
of me, and dragged it some yards away.   There being no stones nor other missiles available, I could
only indulge in a storm of impotent rage, but, notwithstanding the trampling I had undergone, was
able "to keep up with the procession."

The morning was a beautiful one, the sun having
just risen in a clear sky above the mists overhang-
ing and marking the course of the Potomac a mile

to the east, and lighting up the peaks of the Blue Ridge to the west. The country and scenery were not unlike, and equal to the prettiest parts of the Valley. Circling and hovering overhead, calling and answering one another in their peculiarly plaintive notes, as if disturbed by our presence, were the gray plover, a bird I had never before seen. The environment was strikingly peaceful and beautiful, and suggestive of the wish that the Federals, whom we had literally whipped out of their boots and several other articles of attire, and who had now returned to their own country, would remain there, and allow us the same privilege.

But General Lee took a different view of it, and felt that the desired object would be more effectually accomplished by transferring the war into their own territory. So before noon we were again "trekking," and that, too, straight for the Potomac. Orders had again been issued forbidding the cannoneers riding on the caissons anl limbers; but, in crossing the Potomac that day, as the horses were in better shape and the ford smooth, Captain Poague gave us permission to mount and ride over dry-shod. For which breach of discipline he was put under arrest and for several days rode—solemn and downcast—in rear of the battery, with the firm resolve, no doubt, that it was the last act of charity of which he would be guilty during the war. Lieutenant Graham was in command.

CHAPTER XVI

MARYLAND—MY DAY IN FREDERICK CITY

WE were now in Maryland, September 5, 1862. From accounts generally, and more particularly from the opinions expressed by the Maryland members of our battery, we were in eager anticipation of seeing the whole population rise to receive us with open arms, and our depleted ranks swelled by the younger men, impatient for the opportunity to help to achieve Southern independence. The prospect of what was in store for us when we reached Baltimore, as pictured by our boys from that city, filled our minds with such eager yearnings that our impatience to rush in could scarcely be restrained. On the evening of our arrival within the borders of the State, with several companions, I took supper at the house of a Southern sympathizer, who said much to encourage our faith.

In a day of two we were approaching Frederick City. Strict orders had been issued against foraging or leaving the ranks, but Steve Dandridge and I determined to take the bit in our teeth and endeavor to do the town for one day at all hazards. Knowing the officers and provost-guards would be on the alert and hard to evade after the town was reached, we concluded, in order to be safe from their observation, to accomplish that part of our plan beforehand. A field of corn half a mile from the city afforded us good cover till well out of sight. Then, by "taking judicious advantage of the shrubbery," we made our way into a quiet part of the city, and, after scaling a few picket fences, came out into a cross-street remote from the line of march. Steve was the fortunate possessor of a few dollars in greenbacks, my holdings being a like sum in Confederate scrip.

As previously mentioned, our extra baggage—and extra meant all save that worn on our backs—had been left weeks before near the banks of the Rapidan, so that our apparel was now in sad plight. Dandridge had lost his little cadet-cap while on a night march, and supplied its place from the head of a dead Federal at Manassas, his hair still protruding freely, and burnt as "brown as a pretzel bun." The style of my hat was on the other extreme. It had been made to order by a substantial hatter in Lexington, enlisted, and served through the war on one head after another. It was a tall, drab-colored fur of conical shape, with several rows of holes punched around the crown for ventilation. I still wore the lead-colored knit jacket given me by "Buck" Ranson during the Banks campaign. This garment was adorned with a blue stripe near the edges, buttoned close at the throat, and came down well over the hips, fitting after the manner of a shirt. My trousers, issued by the Confederate Quartermaster Department, were fashioned in North

EDWARD A. MOORE
(March, 1862)

Carolina, of a reddish-brown or brick-dust color, part wool and part cotton, elaborate in dimensions about the hips and seat, but tapering and small at the feet, in imitation, as to shape and color, of those worn by Billy Wilson's Zouaves at first Manassas. This is an accurate description of our apparel. Among our fellow-soldiers it attracted no especial attention, as there were many others equally as striking. Very naturally, we were at first eyed with suspicion by the people we met, and when we inquired for a place to get refreshments were directed "down yonder"; in fact anywhere else than where we were.

We soon found a nice little family grocery-store; that is, one kept by a family, including among others two very comely young women. Here we found O'Rourke, an Irishman of our company, who had a talent for nosing out good things—both solids and liquids. We were served with a good repast of native wine, bread, butter, etc.; and, in case we should not have leisure for milder beverages, had a canteen filled with whiskey.

While enjoying our agreeable cheer, a man about thirty years of age came in, he said, to make our acquaintance. He was quite a sharp-looking fellow, with small, keen black eyes, a "glib" tongue, and told us that he was an out-and-out rebel, proud to meet us and ready to oblige. Steve forthwith proposed, as evidence of his good-will, an exchange of headgear. He dilated eloquently on the historic value of his own cap, and, while it did not entirely suit him, exposed as he was to the weather, it would be becoming to a city gentleman, besides reviving the most pleasant associations as a souvenir; and, moreover, the hat the stranger wore was most suitable for a soldier and would do good service to the cause. At length the exchange was made and, Steve having donned the nice black hat, we took our leave. We had scarcely walked a square when our attention was attracted by the sound of rapid footsteps approaching from the rear, and, turning, we saw our new and interesting acquaintance coming at a run. As he passed us, with a high bound he seized the hat from Dandridge's head, threw the cap on the pavement, and disappeared like a flash around the corner.

While seated in a confectionery, enjoying a watermelon we had purchased at a nearby fruitstand, a gentleman came in and insisted on presenting us with a bottle of blackberry brandy, which he recommended as an excellent tonic. We declined his offer, a little suspicious as to the nature of the liquor, but, as he accepted our invitation to partake of our melon, we compromised by joining him in a drink of the brandy, and found it so palatable we regretted not having accepted his proposed present of the whole bottle. Here, with boyish delight, we laid in a supply of confectionery.

Passing along the street soon after this, we were accosted by a venerable-looking gentleman, who stopped us and inquired, very modestly, if there was any way in which he could be of service to us. We could suggest none. He then intimated that we might be a little short of current funds. We could not deny that our funds were somewhat short and not very current. He offered us some greenbacks, of which we accepted a dollar, asking him to try one of our Confederate dollars instead, which he declined to do, but expressed the hope, in a very delicate way, that all of the Confederate soldiers would so conduct themselves as to show the Marylanders of Union proclivities what gentlemen they really were.

Our next experience was rather trying, for me at least, as events will show. Dandridge remembered that he had a lady friend in the city, and proposed that we hunt her up and pay a call. We discussed the subject, I thinking such assurance out of the question; but he said he knew her "like a book," that she had visited at "The Bower," his family home; would excuse our appearance, and be charmed to see us. He knew that, when in Frederick City, she visited at a Mr. Webster's, whose handsome residence we succeeded in locating, and were soon at the door. The bell was answered by a tall, dignified-looking gentleman of about forty-five years, with a full brown beard, who, standing in the half-open door, looked inquiringly as to the object of our visit. Dandridge asked if Miss —— was in. He replied she was, and waited as if inclined to ask, "What business is that of yours?" Dandridge cut the interview short by saying, "My name is Dandridge, and I wish to see her. Come in, Ned." We walked in, and were asked to be seated in the hall. Presently Miss —— appeared. She seemed at first, and doubtless was, somewhat surprised. Dandridge, though, was perfectly natural and at ease, introduced me as if I were a general, and rattled away in his usual style. She informed him that another of his lady friends was in the house, and left us to bring her in. To me the situation was not of the kind I had been seeking and, rising, I said, "Steven, if you have time before the ladies return to manufacture a satisfactory explanation of my absence, do so; otherwise, treat the matter as if you had come alone," and I vanished. Dandridge was invited to remain to dinner, was sumptuously feasted and entertained by the host, and to my astonishment brought me a special invitation to return with him the following day and dine with the household. Other engagements, however, prevented my going.

About four P. M. I met Joe Shaner, of Lexington, and of our battery, on the street. His gun having met with some mishap the day previous, had fallen behind, and had now just come up and passed through the town. Joe was wofully dejected, and deplored missing, as one would have imagined, the opportunity of his life—a day in such a city, teeming with all that was good. But little time now remained before evening roll-call, when each must give an account of himself. He was hungry, tired, and warm, and I felt it my duty to comfort him as far as possible. I asked him how he would like a taste of whiskey. "It's just what I need," was his quiet reply, and before I had time to get the strap off of my shoulder he dropped on one knee on the curb-stone and had my canteen upside down to his mouth, oblivious of those passing by. He had no money, but, being a messmate, I invested the remnant of my change for his benefit, but found it necessary to include a weighty watermelon, to make out his load to camp.

The next acquaintance I met was George Bedinger, whom I found, clad *à la mode,* standing in a hotel-door with an expression of calm satisfaction on his face. As I came up to him, carrying my recent purchases tied in a bandana handkerchief, and stood before him, he scanned me from head to foot, said not a word, but fell back with a roar of laughter. Gay, brilliant Bedinger, whose presence imparted an electric touch to those around him; I shall ne'er see his like again!

The sun was now setting; camp was two miles away. Thither I set out, cheered by the assurance that, whatever punishment befell, I had had a day. Arriving there, my apprehensions were relieved, possibly because offenses of the kind were too numerous to be handled conveniently. About dusk that evening a free fight between the members of our company and those of Raine's battery, of Lynchburg, was with difficulty prevented by the officers of the companies, who rushed in with their sabers. The Alleghany Roughs, hearing the commotion, one of their men cried out, "Old Rockbridge may need us! Come on, boys, let's see them through!" And on they came.

We spent two or three days in a clean, fresh camp in this fertile country, supplied with an abundance of what it afforded. At noon each day apple-dumplings could be seen dancing in the boiling camp-kettles, with some to spare for a visitor, provided he could furnish his own plate.

On the tenth came orders "to hitch up," but to our surprise and disappointment we turned back in the direction from which we had come, instead of proceeding toward Baltimore and Washington, and the realization of our bright hopes. We crossed the Potomac at Williamsport, thirty miles northwest, but not dry-shod. Thence southwest into Jefferson County, West Virginia.

CHAPTER XVII

RETURN TO VIRGINIA—INVESTMENT AND CAPTURE OF HARPER'S FERRY

At Harper's Ferry there was a considerable force of the enemy, which place was now evidently the object of the expedition, and which we approached soon after noon on the thirteenth. After the usual delays required in getting troops deployed, our battery was posted on an elevated ridge northwest of Bolivar Heights, the stronghold of the Federals, and confronting their bold array of guns directed toward us.

We opened fire and were answered, but without apparent effect on either side. This was late in the afternoon, and night came on before anything was accomplished. The situation of Harper's Ferry is too well known to require description. Only by a view of its surroundings from some adjacent eminence can one form an idea of its beauty. As we stood by our guns on the morning of the fifteenth we were aware of what had been in progress for the investment of the place, and now, that having been accomplished, we awaited with interest the general assault that was soon to follow.

Directly on the opposite side of Bolivar Heights from where we stood was Loudoun, or Virginia

Heights, the extreme north end of the Blue Ridge in Virginia, at the base of which flowed the Shenandoah River, and now held by our artillery, as were also Maryland Heights, across the Potomac, while various lines of infantry lay concealed along the banks of both rivers and intervening valleys, completely enveloping the Federal position.

The morning was still and clear, giving us a full view of the lines of the lofty mountains. Simultaneously the great circle of artillery opened, all firing to a common center, while the clouds of smoke, rolling up from the tops of the various mountains, and the thunder of the guns reverberating among them, gave the idea of so many volcanoes.

The contrast between the conditions and the scene presented as I viewed the surroundings five years later, during Christmas, 1867, is too striking to be forgotten.

On the face of the country, mountain, field and forest lay a deep snow and on this a sleet had fallen, encasing every tree, shrub and fence in a glassy coating; and as I sped along the highway behind jingling sleigh-bells, seated by a young lady uncommon fair, the morning sun blazing through the mountain gorge cut by the rivers, and reflected from myriads of sparkling icy prisms, made a scene of dazzling beauty.

The fire of the Federals in the unequal contest made no perceptible impression, not even on the lines of infantry which had begun closing in from all sides for the final charge. Before they (the infantry) were within musket range, a horseman bearing a large piece of tent-cloth swept along the crest of Bolivar Heights. The doubtful color of the flag displayed prevented an immediate cessation of the Confederate fire. It proved to be in token of surrender, but after its appearance I saw a shot from our second piece strike so near a horseman riding at speed along the heights as to envelop horse and rider in its smoke and dust.

The whole affair, devoid, as it was, of ordinary danger, was one of thrilling interest. Our commanding position gave us a full view of the extensive and varied terrain, a thing of rare occurrence to other than general officers. In addition to this, the fact that we had defeated our antagonists, usually in superior numbers, in battle after battle throughout a long campaign, tended to confirm us in the opinion that we could down them every time, and that the contest must, at no distant day, end in our favor. The number of troops surrendered was 11,500, with seventy-three pieces of artillery, sufficient to supply our batteries for some time. It was comparatively a bloodless victory, though the commanding officer, Colonel Miles, was killed at the last moment, and the terms of surrender arranged by General White, who had fallen back to this place from Martinsburg. I saw their artillery as it was driven out and turned over to us, supplied with most excellent equipments, and horses sleek and fat.

As some time would be consumed in handling the prisoners and the transfer of arms and stores, I set out in the afternoon for Charlestown, and, as usual, went to my friends—the Ransons. After a refreshing bath I donned a clean white shirt and a pair of light-checked trousers, and was ready to discuss the events of the campaign with General Lindsay Walker, who was also a guest of the house. About nine o'clock at night I was joined by Dandridge, who had been met in the town by his mother and sisters from "The Bower," and, with light hearts and full haversacks, we set out for camp seven miles distant.

The Ranson family has several times been mentioned in these pages, as their home was a place where, when hungry, I was fed and, when naked, clothed. The oldest son, Tom, now a lawyer in Staunton, Virginia, was my schoolfellow and classmate at college when a boy in Lexington. After receiving a wound at Cross Keys in June, 1862, when a lieutenant in the Fifty-second Virginia Regiment, which incapacitated him for further service in the infantry, he enlisted in the cavalry. By reason of his familiarity with the topography of the country about Harper's Ferry and the lower portion of the Valley, together with his indomitable pluck and steady nerve, he was often employed as a scout, and in this capacity frequently visited his home near Charlestown. The residence, situated, as it was, a quarter of a mile from and overlooking the town, was approached by a wide avenue leading by a gentle ascent to the front gate, which stood about seventy-five yards from the house. Owing to the commanding view thus afforded, it was a favorite place for a Federal picket-post, so that, while a dangerous place for a rebel soldier to venture, it offered many facilities for obtaining valuable information. On one occasion young Ranson spent three days in this home while the Federal pickets were on constant watch day and night at the front gate opening into the lawn, and went in and out of the house at their convenience. Moreover, the negro servants of the family knew of "Marse Tom's" presence, but looked and acted negro ignorance to perfection when catechised.

When standing at a front window one afternoon Tom saw a lady friend of the family approaching the house from the town. On reaching the front gate she, of course, was stopped by the sentinel and, after a parley, refused admittance and required to retrace her steps. Two hours later, much to their surprise, she appeared in the family-room and sank down completely exhausted, having entered the house by a rear door, which she had reached after making a detour of a mile or more to escape the vigilance of the videttes in front. After recovering breath she unburdened herself of her load, which consisted, in part, of a pair of long-legged cavalry boots, late issues of Northern newspapers, etc. This load she had carried suspended from her waist and concealed under the large hoop-skirt then worn by ladies. The newspapers and information of large bodies of Federal troops being hurried by rail past Harper's Ferry were delivered by young Ranson to General Lee on the following day.

Throughout the preceding day, while occupied about Harper's Ferry, we heard heavy cannonading across the Maryland border, apparently eight or ten miles from us. This had increased in volume, and by sunset had evidently advanced toward us, as the sound of musketry was distinctly heard. It proved to be an attack on Gen. D. H. Hill's division and other commands occupying the South Mountain passes. After stubborn resistance the Confederates had been forced to yield. So on reaching camp toward midnight, after our visit to Charlestown, we were not surprised to find the battery preparing to move. With scarcely an hour's delay we were again on the march, heading for Maryland. We arrived at Shepherdstown before dawn, and while halting in the road for half an hour Henry Lewis, driver at my gun, overcome with sleep, fell sprawling from his horse, rousing those about him from a similar condition.

CHAPTER XVIII

HALF a mile below the town we forded the Potomac for the third time, and by the middle of the afternoon were on the outskirts of Sharpsburg, four miles from the river. On the opposite, or east, side of this village are Antietam creek and valley; a mile from the creek and parallel to it was a heavily wooded mountain. It is not my design to attempt a description of the battle which was fought on this ground on the following day, generally conceded to have been the fiercest of the war, but only to mention what came under my observation or was especially associated therewith.

The unusual activity and aggressiveness on the part of General McClellan, as evidenced by the fierce attacks made on our forces in the South Mountain passes for the two preceding days, were explained by his being in possession of General Lee's order to his subordinates. This order, or a copy of it, which contained directions for the movements of the various portions of the Confederate army, including the investment of Harper's Ferry, had been lost or disposed of by some one in Frederick City, and when this place was occupied, on September 13, by the Federals, was delivered to General McClellan. Thus

147

acquainted with the location and movements of each division of the Confederate army, which was scattered over a wide territory and separated by a river and rugged mountains, it seems surprising that with his army of 90,000 men he should not have practically destroyed General Lee's army of 40,000. General Lee, however, was informed early on the morning of the fourteenth that a copy of his order had fallen into the hands of General McClellan.

This was done by a citizen of Frederick City who happened to be present when General McClellan received it and heard him express satisfaction over such a stroke of luck. This citizen at once went to work to inform General Lee, which task he accomplished by passing through the Federal lines during the night and informing General Stuart, who forthwith communicated it to General Lee, who lost no time in moving heaven and earth—the former by prayer, we assume; the latter by his authority over men—to meet the emergency. Results proved how wonderfully he succeeded.

As we moved past the town we saw neither any of our troops nor those of the enemy, and heard no firing. Although there was complete absence of the usual prelude to battle, still the apprehension came over us that something serious in that line was not very remote, either in time or place. The commanders of both armies were conscious of the importance of the impending contest, which perhaps explains the extreme caution they exercised.

After passing through a piece of woodland, we entered a small field and came in distinct view of two blue lines of battle, drawn up one in rear of the other. On these we at once opened fire, and were answered very promptly by a Federal battery in the same quarter. While thus engaged we had a visitor in the person of a young fellow who had just been commissioned a lieutenant, having previously been an orderly at brigade headquarters. Feeling his newly acquired importance, he spurred his horse around among the guns, calling out, "Let 'em have it!" and the like, until, seeing our disgust at his impertinent encouragement, and that we preferred a chance to let him have it, he departed. Our next visitor came in a different guise, and by a hint of another kind was quickly disposed of. He, a man of unusually large size, with sword dangling at his side, came bounding from our right at a full run. A large log a few steps in our rear was his goal as a place of safety, and over it he leaped and was instantly concealed behind it. He had scant time to adjust himself before the log was struck a crashing blow by a solid shot. He reappeared as part of the upheaval; but, regaining his feet, broke for the woods with the speed of a quarter-horse, and with a greater confidence in distance than in logs.

It was now dark, and our range had been accurately gotten. After each discharge of our opponent's guns, what appeared to be a harmless spark of fire, immovable as a star, repeatedly de-

ceived us. It was the burning fuse in the head of
the shell which, coming straight toward us, seemed
stationary until the shell shot by or burst. Four
young mules drawing our battery-forge were
stampeded by these shells and ran off through the
woods, thus affording Pleasants, our blacksmith,
entertainment for the rest of the night.

Firing ceased on both sides at about eight o'clock,
and we passed through the woods to our left and
went into park on the opposite side. Still feeling
the comfort of my clean clothes, I enjoyed a quiet
night's rest on the top of a caisson, little heeding
the gentle rain which fell on my face. Our bivouac
was immediately by the "Straw-stacks," which
have been so generally referred to as landmarks in
this battle, and which were located in the open
ground near the forest which extended to the Dunkard church. About seven o'clock next morning,
while standing with horses hitched and awaiting
orders, no engagement so far having taken place
near us, a shell of great size burst with a terrific
report. One fragment of it mortally wounded Sam
Moore, a driver of my gun, while another piece cut
off the forefoot of one of the horses in the team.
We soon transferred his harness to another horse
which we hitched in his stead and, as we went off
at a trot, the crippled horse took his place close by
where he was accustomed to work, and kept alongside on three legs until his suffering was relieved
by a bullet in the brain.

We had moved, to get out of range of missiles, but the place to which we had just come was not an improvement. While standing with the gun in front turned in file at right angles to those following, a twenty-pound shell swept by the six drivers and their teams in the rear, just grazing them, then striking the ground, ricocheted almost between the forward driver and his saddle as he threw himself forward on the horse's neck. I mention this in contrast with an occurrence later in the day, when one shell killed or wounded all of the six horses in a team, together with their three drivers.

Fighting along the line of four miles had become general—done on our side chiefly by infantry. Jackson's corps occupied the left with a thin line of men, and from it there was already a stream of stragglers. Jackson, while sitting nearby on his horse, watching the battle, was approached by a lad of about thirteen years, who for some time had been one of his orderlies. He began talking in a very animated manner, pointing the while to different parts of the field. Jackson kept his eyes on the ground, but gave close attention to what was said. The boy was Charles Randolph, and soon after this became a cadet at the Virginia Military Institute, and at the battle of New Market was left on the field for dead. Fourteen years after the war, while visiting in a neighboring county, I was introduced to a Reverend Mr. Randolph, and, seeing the resemblance to the soldier-boy, I asked him about Sharpsburg, recalling the incident, and found he was the lad.

The straggling already mentioned continually increased, and seemed to give General Jackson great concern. He endeavored, with the aid of his staff officers who were present and the members of our company, to stop the men and turn them back, but without the least effect; claiming, as they did, the want of ammunition and the usual excuses. The marvel was, how those remaining in line could have withstood the tremendous odds against them; but, from accounts, the enemy suffered the same experience, and in a greater degree. Up to this time, with the exception of a return of our battery to the Dunkard church, where we had fought the evening before, we had done nothing. At about ten o'clock the indications were that if reinforcements could not be promptly had serious consequences would follow. But just after our return from the church to General Jackson's place of observation we saw a long column of troops approaching from the right. This was McLaw's division of Longstreet's corps, which had just reached the field. Their coming was most opportune, and but a short time elapsed before the comparative quiet was interrupted—first by volleys, followed by a continuous roar of battle.

Our battery was now ordered to the left of our line, and on the way thither joined Raine's battery, of Lynchburg, and a battery of Louisianians—eleven guns in all. Besides the ordinary number of guns accompanying infantry, we had to contend with about thirty 32-pounders on the high ground in the rear and entirely commanding that part of the field. In view of the superior odds against us, our orders were to hold our positions as long as possible, then to move to our left and occupy new ones. Why such instructions were given was soon explained, as the ground over which we passed, and where we stopped to fire, was strewn with the dead horses and the wrecks of guns and caissons of the batteries which had preceded us. By the practice thus afforded, the Federal batteries had gotten a perfect range, and by the time our guns were unlimbered we were enveloped in the smoke and dust of bursting shells, and the air was alive with flying iron. At most of the positions we occupied on this move it was the exception when splinters and pieces of broken rails were not flying from the fences which stood in our front, hurled by shot and shell.

Working in the lead of one of the Louisiana battery teams was a horse that frequently attracted my admiration. A rich blood-bay in color, with flowing black mane and tail, as he swept around in the various changes with wide, glowing nostrils and flecked with foam, in my eyes he came well up to the description of the war-horse whose "neck was clothed with thunder."

Moving as we had been doing, toward the left of our line, we passed beyond that portion held by regular infantry commands into what was defended by a mere show of force when scarcely any existed. In charge of it was Gen. J. E. B. Stuart, who demonstrated on this occasion his ability to accomplish what it would seem impossible for one man to do. With a few skeleton regiments supplied with numerous flags which he posted to show over the crests of the ridges in our rear, as if there were men in proportion, he himself took command of a line of sharpshooters in our front. This skirmish-line was composed of stragglers he had gathered up, and whom he had transformed from a lot of shirkers into a band of heroes. With black plume floating, cheering and singing, back and forth along the line he swept.

The Federals confronting us in the three blue lines could not have been less than 8,000 men, who, with their powerful artillery, should have utterly overwhelmed the scant numbers handled by Stuart. As the blue lines would start forward, calling to our artillery to pour in the shells again, he would urge on his sharpshooters to meet them half-way. The failure of a strong force of Federals to advance farther is explained, no doubt, by the fact that two of their army corps and one division had suffered terribly a short time before near the same ground.

Colonel Allan states, in his "Army of Northern Virginia, 1862," page 409, "Of Hooker's and Mansfield's corps, and of Sedgwick's division, was nothing left available for further operations"; and General Palfrey, the Northern historian, says, "In less

time than it takes to tell it, the ground was strewn
with the bodies of the dead and wounded, while the
unwounded were moving off rapidly to the north."
(Palfrey, "Antietam and Fredericksburg," page
87.)

While engaged in one of these artillery duels a
thirty-two-pound shot tore by the gun and struck
close by Henry Rader, a driver, who was lying on
the ground, holding the lead-horses at the limber.
The shell tore a trench alongside of him, and hoisted
him horizontally from the ground. As he staggered off, dazed by the shock, the horses swung
around to run, when young R. E. Lee, Jr., with
bare arms and face begrimed with powder, made
a dash from the gun, seized the bridle of each of the
leaders at the mouth, and brought them back into
position before the dust had cleared away.

In the constant changes from knoll to knoll, in
accordance with orders to "move when the fire became too hot," some of the batteries with us withdrew, perhaps prematurely. In this way the Rockbridge guns were left to receive the whole of the
enemy's fire. In just such a situation as this, it not
being to our liking, I asked Lieutenant Graham if
we should pull out when the others did. Before he
could answer the question a shell burst at our gun,
from which an iron ball an inch in diameter struck
me on the right thigh-joint, tearing and carrying
the clothes in to the bone. I fell, paralyzed with
excruciating pain. Graham rode off, thinking I was

killed, as he afterward told me. The pain soon subsided, and I was at first content to lie still; but, seeing the grass and earth around constantly torn up,
and sometimes thrown on me, I made fruitless
efforts to move. The strict orders against assisting
the wounded prevented my being carried off until
the firing had ceased, when I was taken back about
fifty yards and my wound examined by two sur-
geons from the skeleton regiments, who treated me
with the utmost kindness, thinking, perhaps, from
my clean white shirt, that I was an officer. An hour
later my gun came by, and I was put on a caisson
and hauled around for an hour or two more.

It was about this time that what was left of the
battery was seen by General Lee, and the interview
between him and his son took place. To give an
idea of the condition of the battery, I quote from
"Recollections and Letters of General Lee," by
R. E. Lee, Jr., page 77:

"As one of the Army of Northern Virginia I
occasionally saw the Commander-in-Chief, or passed
the headquarters close enough to recognize him and
members of his staff; but a private soldier in Jackson's corps did not have much time during that campaign for visiting, and until the battle of Sharpsburg I had no opportunity of speaking to him. On
that occasion our battery had been severely handled,
losing many men and horses. Having three guns
disabled, we were ordered to withdraw and, while
moving back, we passed General Lee and several of

his staff grouped on a little knoll near the road.
Having no definite orders where to go, our captain,
seeing the commanding General, halted us and rode
over to get some instructions. Some others and myself went along to see and hear. General Lee was
dismounted with some of his staff around him, a
courier holding his horse. Captain Poague, commanding our battery, the Rockbridge Artillery, saluted, reported our condition, and asked for instructions. The General listened patiently, looked at us,
his eyes passing over me without any sign of recognition, and then ordered Captain Poague to take the
most serviceable horses and men, man the unin-
jured gun, send the disabled part of his command
back to refit, and report to the front for duty. As
Poague turned to go, I went up to speak to my
father. When he found out who I was he con-
gratulated me on being well and unhurt. I then
said, 'General, are you going to send us in again?'
'Yes, my son,' he replied, with a smile, 'you all must
do what you can to help drive these people back.'
In a letter to Mrs. Lee, General Lee says, 'I have
not laid eyes on Rob since I saw him in the battle
of Sharpsburg, going in with a single gun of his,
for the second time, after his company had been
withdrawn in consequence of three of its guns having been disabled. . . .' "

Held by a companion on the caisson, as it was
driven toward our right, jolting over the partly
torn-down fences and exposed to far-reaching mis-

siles, I had an opportunity of seeing other portions of the battlefield. We stopped for a time on the ridge overlooking the village almost enveloped in the flames of burning buildings, while flocks of terrified pigeons, driven hither and thither by the screaming and bursting shells, flew round and round in the clouds of smoke. In hearing, from beyond and to the left of the village, was the fighting at "Bloody Lane," a sunken road which was almost filled with the dead of both sides when the day closed. As was also that at "Burnside Bridge," a mile southeast of the town, for the possession of which Burnside's corps and Toombs's Georgians contended till late in the afternoon. I was not averse to leaving this scene when the disabled caisson proceeded, and reached the pike.

A mile farther on I was deposited on the roadside, near the brigade field-hospital; and, completely exhausted, was carried into the yard of a neat brick cottage by two stalwart Alleghany Roughs and laid beside their captain, John Carpenter. The place, inside and out, was filled with wounded men. Carpenter insisted on my taking the last of his two-ounce vial of whiskey, which wonderfully revived me. Upon inquiry, he told me he had been shot through the knee by a piece of shell and that the surgeons wanted to amputate his leg, but, calling my attention to a pistol at his side, said, "You see that? It will not be taken off while I can pull a trigger." He entirely recovered, and led his battery into the next battle, where he was again severely wounded. That the history of the four Carpenter brothers of Alleghany County, Virginia, has not been recorded is a misfortune. As already mentioned, Joe, the oldest, and captain of the Alleghany Rough Battery, was mortally wounded near us at Cedar Mountain. John, who succeeded him as captain, after being wounded at Sharpsburg, was again wounded at Fredericksburg in 1862, where he was twice carried from the field, and as often worked his way back to his gun. In Early's campaign in 1864 he lost his right arm. In the same campaign his next younger brother, Ben, lieutenant in the same company, was shot through the lungs. The wounds of neither had healed when they received news, at their home, of the surrender at Appomattox. Mounting their horses, they set out for Gen. Joe Johnston's army in North Carolina, but, on arriving at Lexington, Virginia, heard of the surrender of that army. The fourth and youngest brother lost a leg near the close of the war. Like all true heroes, their modesty was as striking as their courage and patriotism.

On the following day at our hospital the heap of amputated legs and arms increased in size until it became several feet in height, while the two armies lay face to face, like two exhausted monsters, each waiting for the other to strike.

About sundown that afternoon I was put in an ambulance with S. R. Moore, of the College company, who was in a semi-conscious state, having been struck on the brow, the ball passing out back of the ear. The distance to Shepherdstown was only three miles, but the slow progress of innumerable trains of wagons and impedimenta generally, converging at the one ford of the Potomac, delayed our arrival until dawn the next morning. About sunrise we were carried into an old deserted frame house and assigned to the bare floor for beds. My brother David, whose gun had remained on picket duty on this side of the river, soon found me, and at once set about finding means to get me away. The only conveyance available was George Bedinger's mother's carriage, but my brother's horse—the same brute that had robbed me of my bedding at Leesburg—now refused to work.

The booming of cannon and bursting of shells along the river at the lower end of the town admonished us that our stay in the desolate old house must be short, and, as brigade after brigade marched by the door, the apprehension that "they in whose wars I had borne my part" would soon "have all passed by," made me very wretched. As a last resort, I was lifted upon the back of this same obstreperous horse and, in great pain, rode to the battery, which was camped a short distance from the town.

S. R. Moore was afterward taken to the Bedingers' residence, where he remained in the enemy's

R. T. BARTON

lines until, with their permission, he was taken home by his father some weeks later.

David Barton, a former member of our company, but now in command of Cutshaw's battery, kindly sent his ambulance, with instructions that I be taken to his father's house in Winchester, which place, in company with a wounded man of his battery, I reached on the following day. At Mr. Barton's I found my cousin and theirs, Robert Barton, of Rockbridge, on sick-leave, and a Doctor Grammer, who dressed my wound; and, although unable to leave my bed, I intensely enjoyed the rest and kindness received in that hospitable home, which was repeatedly made desolate by the deaths of its gallant sons who fell in battle.

Marshall, the eldest, and lieutenant in artillery, was killed on the outskirts of Winchester in May, 1862. David, the third son, whom I have just mentioned, was killed in December of the same year. Strother, the second son, lost a leg at Chancellorsville and died soon after the war; and Randolph, the fourth son, captain on the staff of the Stonewall Brigade, and now a distinguished lawyer in Baltimore, was seven times wounded, while Robert, a member of our battery, and a gallant soldier, was the only one of the five brothers in the service who survived the war unscathed. Our mutual cousin, Robert Barton of the Rockbridge Cavalry, was shot through the lungs in Early's Valley campaign, and left within the enemy's lines, where, nursed by his sister, his life hung in the balance for many days.

The following copy of a letter from Gen. J. E. B. Stuart to Miss Virginia Barton is of interest:

"CENTERVILLE, Feb. 7, 1862.

"MY DEAR MISS BARTON:

"I received your note just as I was upon the point of granting your brother a furlough.   It greatly enhances the pleasure it afforded me to grant it, to know how dear a sister he has to receive him at home.

"I avail myself of this opportunity to express my very high appreciation of the conspicuous gallantry he has displayed on all occasions, and to assure you that he is a cavalier of whom a sister and a country may be justly proud.

"Hoping when the war is ended and peace once more smiles on old Virginia, to do myself the honor to make the acquaintance of the fair young Virginia, I am very truly and sincerely,

"Your well-wisher,

"J. E. B. STUART."

After a sojourn of a few days, leave to go home was given me by the department surgeon, and at four o'clock in the morning, with young Bolling, Barton and Reid serving as my crutches (on their way to the Virginia Military Institute), I was put in the stage-coach at the front door and driven to the hotel, where several Baltimoreans, who were returning from Northern prisons, got in. One of them was especially noticeable, as his face was much pitted by smallpox, and with his Confederate uniform he wore a wide-brimmed straw hat. They were a jolly set, and enlivened the journey no little. A square or two farther on, two wounded officers came from a house at which we stopped, and in an authoritative manner demanded seats, inside, all of which were occupied. They said they were officers in a celebrated command and expected corresponding consideration. The fellow with the hat told them his party was just from Fort Delaware, where little distinction was paid to rank, but if they required exalted positions they ought to get on top of the coach. The officers said they were wounded and could not climb up. "I was wounded, too— mortally," came from under the hat. After joking them sufficiently, the Baltimoreans kindly gave up their seats and mounted to the top.

At the towns at which we stopped to change horses, the boys who collected around were entertained with wonderful stories by our friends from Baltimore. Just outside of one of these stopping-places, we passed an old gentleman, probably refugeeing, who wore a tall beaver hat and rode a piebald pony. To the usual crowd of lads who had gathered around, they said they were going to give a show in the next town and wanted them all to come, would give them free tickets, and each a hatful of "goobers"; then pointing to the old gentleman on the spotted pony, who had now ridden up, said, "Ah, there is our clown; he can give you full particulars." One hundred and thirty miles from the battle-field of Sharpsburg the dawn of the second day of our journey showed again the procession of wounded men, by whom we had been passing all night and who had bivouacked along the road as darkness overtook them.

They were now astir, bathing each other's wounds. The distance from Winchester to Staunton is ninety-six miles, and the trip was made by our stage in twenty-six hours, with stops only long enough to change horses.

From nine to ten o'clock in the night I was utterly exhausted, and felt that I could not go a mile farther alive; but rallied, and reached Staunton at six o'clock in the morning, having been twenty-six hours on the way. Here Sam Lyle and Joe Chester, of the College company, detailed as a provost-guard, cared for me until the next day, when another stage-ride of thirty-six miles brought me to Lexington and home. With the aid of a crutch I was soon able to get about, but four months passed before I was again fit for duty, and from the effects of the wound I am lame to this day.

Since going into the service in March, 1862, six months before, I had been in nine pitched battles, about the same number of skirmishes, and had marched more than one thousand miles—and this, too, with no natural taste for war.

CHAPTER XIX

ON December 13, 1862, the great first battle of
Fredericksburg had been fought, in which four men
—Montgomery, McCalpin, Fuller and Beard—in
my detachment had been killed, and others wounded,
while the second piece, standing close by, did not
lose a man. This section of the battery was posted
in the flat, east of the railroad. As I was not present in this battle I will insert an account recently
given me by Dr. Robert Frazer, a member of the
detachment, who was severely wounded at the time:

"First battle of Fredericksburg, December 13,
1862.—We reached the field a little after sunrise,
having come up during the night from Port Royal,
where we had been engaging the enemy's gunboats.
The first section, under Lieutenant Graham, went
immediately into action in front of Hamilton's
Crossing.

"In conjunction with Stuart's horse artillery it
was our mission to meet Burnside's movement
against General Lee's right wing, resting on the
Rappahannock. With the exception of brief intervals, to let the guns cool, we ceased firing only once
during the entire day, and this was to move about

a hundred yards for a more effective position. Excepting the few minutes this occupied, our guns and limber-chests remained in the same position all day, the caissons plying steadily between the ordnance-train and the battle line, to keep up the stock of ammunition. I do not recall the number of casualties, but our losses were heavy. When we came to make the change of position mentioned above, more than half the horses were unable to take a single step. One of the drivers, Fuller, was lying on the ground, his head toward the enemy. A shell entered the crown of his head and exploded in his body! Not long after this I heard some one calling me, and, looking back, I saw 'Doc' Montgomery prostrate. I ran to him and, stooping at his side, began to examine his wound. 'There is nothing you can do for me,' he said, 'I am mortally wounded, and can live but a little while. Take a message for my mother.' (His mother was a widow.) 'When the battle is over, write and tell her how I died—at my post—like a man—and ready to give my life for the cause. Now, Frazer, pray for me.' When the brief prayer was ended I resumed my place at the gun. It was about this time, I think, that Pelham came up and said, 'Well, you men stand killing better than any I ever saw.' A little later, just after sunset, I received two severe wounds myself, one of them disabling my right arm for life; and so I had to commit brave 'Doc's' dying message for his mother to other hands."

The third and fourth pieces, twenty-pound Parrott guns, were on the hill west of the railroad, and there Lieutenant Baxter McCorkle, Randolph Fairfax and Arthur Robinson were killed, and Edward Alexander lost an arm. Lieut.-Col. Lewis Coleman, professor of Latin at the University of Virginia, second in command of the battalion, while standing by this gun received a mortal wound. This section of the battery was exposed to a fire unsurpassed in fierceness during the war. The ground, when it arrived, was already strewn with dead horses and wrecked batteries, and two horses that were standing, with holes in their heads through which daylight could be seen, were instantly killed by other shots intended for our guns.

Captain Poague has since told me that the orders General Jackson gave him as he came to the place were, "to fire on the enemy's artillery till it became too hot for him, and then to turn his guns on their infantry," and that he, Poague, had stated this in his official report, and the chief of artillery of the corps, before forwarding the report, had asked him if he was sure that these were General Jackson's orders. He told him he was. The report was then endorsed and so forwarded.

The scene, as described at the close of this battle near nightfall, was a melancholy one. As the two sections of the battery, which had separated and gone to different portions of the field in the morning—the one to the heights, the other to the plain

—met again, on the caissons of each were borne the dead bodies of those of their number who had fallen, the wounded, and the harness stripped from the dead horses. The few horses that had survived, though scarcely able to drag the now empty ammunition-chests, were thus again burdened.

After going into bivouac and the dead had been buried, to clear the ground for a renewal of the battle on the following day, the wagon-horses had to be brought into requisition. These were driven in pairs to the position on the bluff and, as lights would attract the fire of the enemy, the dead horses had to be found in the darkness, and with chains dragged to the rear. The approach of the first instalment to a line of infantry, through which it had to pass and who were roused from sleep by the rattling of chains and the dragging of the ponderous bodies through brush and fallen timber, created no little excitement, and a wide berth was given the gruesome procession. By midnight the work had been accomplished.

At dawn of the following day a fresh detachment of men and horses having been furnished by another battery for the fourth piece, our battery again went into position. There it remained inactive throughout the day, while the enemy's dead within our lines were being buried by their own men under flag of truce. On the night which followed, as the two armies lay under arms, confronting each other, a display of the aurora borealis, of

Winter Quarters, Mess No. 12, Rockbridge Artillery, 1862-3

surpassing splendor and beauty, was witnessed. At such times, from time immemorial, "shooting-stars," comets, and the movements of the heavenly bodies have been observed with profoundest interest as presaging good or evil. On this occasion, with the deep impress of what had just been experienced and the apprehension of an even more determined conflict on the day next to dawn, it can readily be imagined that minds naturally prone to superstition were thrilled with emotions and conjectures aroused by the sight. At any rate, these "northern lights," reinforced by the memory of the fearful carnage so recently suffered, seem to have been interpreted as a summons home—as the Northern hosts, like the shifting lights, had vanished from view when daylight appeared.

In January, 1863, with William McClintic, of our company, I returned to the army, which was in winter-quarters near Guiney's Station in Caroline County.

After arriving in a box-car at this station, about midnight, during a pouring rain, we found one section of the battery camped three miles from Port Royal. The other section, to which I belonged, was on picket twelve miles beyond—at Jack's Hill, overlooking Port Tobacco Bay. The section near Port Royal had comfortable winter-quarters on a hillside and was well sheltered in pine woods. The picture on the opposite page, is a copy from the original, and a perfect representation by Edward Hyde, who, with William Bolling, Thomas McCorkle, William McClintic, A. S. Dandridge, G. W. Stewart, David Moore, and myself, constituted the mess. The homes of the other messes, at intervals, near. The tent on the left was our sleeping apartment, accommodating six men; the other two occupied a Yankee tent-fly, not shown in the picture. We slept three in a bed; when weary of lying on one side, the word to turn over was "when," and the movement was executed simultaneously and with military precision. The other structure was our kitchen and dining-room, a semi-"dugout," with the fireplace in the earthen wall. The little box attached to a log contained our table-ware, if we had had a table, and was just above the mess-chest. We had two meals a day, consisting usually of meat and biscuit. Generally we had coffee, either genuine or rye, similar in flavor to "postum."

When the number of biscuit turned out happened not to be a multiple of eight, say fifty-seven, every man in the mess took into account the odd one, and to get through with the seven allotted to him, without appearing over-anxious to secure it, with becoming propriety, and aware, too, that every other man had the same ambition, brought into play an exercise of talent that was not uninteresting. An extra draught of coffee left in the pot was subject to similar consideration and fell to the lot of him whose throat could stand the highest degree of temperature. More than once there were evidences that the boiling process had not entirely ceased until after it was swallowed. The plantation adjoining the one on which we were camped was owned by a gentleman named Garrett, and at his barn Wilkes Booth, who assassinated President Lincoln, was afterwards overtaken and killed.

As most of my mess were in this section, I was allowed to remain until the contents of my box brought from home were consumed. One night soon after my arrival, while making a visit to members of another mess, Abner Arnold, one of my hosts, pointing to several large, dark stains on the tarpaulin which served as the roof of their shanty, said, "Have you any idea what discolored those places?" As I had not, he said, "That's your blood; that is the caisson-cover on which you were hauled around at Sharpsburg—and neither rain nor snow can wash it out."

The infantry of the Stonewall Brigade was in camp seven miles from us, toward the railroad. Having ridden there one morning for our mail, I met two men in one of their winter-quarters' streets. One of them, wearing a citizen's overcoat, attracted my attention. Then, noticing the scars on his face, I recognized my former messmate, Wash. Stuart, on his return to the battery for the first time since his fearful wound at Winchester the preceding May. His companion was Capt. Willie Randolph, of the Second Virginia Regiment, both of whom will be mentioned later.

The chief sport of the troops in their winter-quarters was snowballing, which was conducted on regular military principles. Two brigades would sometimes form in line of battle, commanded by their officers, and pelt each other without mercy. In one such engagement a whole brigade was driven pell-mell through its camp, and their cooking utensils captured by their opponents.

Once a week quite regularly an old negro man came to our camp with a wagon-load of fine oysters from Tappahannock. It was interesting to see some of the men from our mountains, who had never seen the bivalve before, trying to eat them, and hear their comments. Our custom was to buy anything to eat that came along, and so they had invested their Confederate notes in oysters. One of them gave some of my messmates an account of the time his mess had had with their purchases. When it was proposed that they sell their supply to us, he said, "No, we are not afraid to tackle anything, and we've made up our minds to eat what we've got on hand, if it takes the hair off."

While in this camp, although it was after a five-months' absence, I invariably waked about two minutes before my time to go on guard, having slept soundly during the rest of the four hours. One officer, always finding me awake, asked if I ever slept at all. The habit did not continue, and had not been experienced before. An instance of the opposite extreme I witnessed here in an effort to rouse Silvey, who was generally a driver. After getting him on his feet, he was shaken, pulled, and dragged around a blazing fire, almost scorching him, until the guard-officer had to give him up. If feigning, it was never discovered.

The contents of my box having long since been consumed, I, with several others, was sent, under command of Lieut. Cole Davis, to my section at Jack's Hill. There we were quartered in some negro cabins on this bleak hill, over which the cold winds from Port Tobacco Bay had a fair sweep. On my return from the sentinel's beat one snowy night I discovered, by the dim firelight, eight or ten sheep in our cabin, sheltering from the storm. The temptation, with such an opportunity, to stir up a panic, was hard to resist. But, fearing the loss of an eye or other injury to the prostrate sleepers on the dirt floor, by the hoof of a bucking sheep, I concluded to forego the fun. After a stay of several weeks we were ordered back to the other section, much to our delight. In that barren region, with scant provender and protected from the weather by a roof of cedar-brush, our horses had fared badly, and showed no disposition to pull when hitched to the guns that were held tight in the frozen mud. To one of the drivers, very tall and long of limb, who was trying in vain with voice and spur to urge his team to do its best, our Irish wit, Tom Martin, called out, "Pull up your frog-legs, Tomlin, if you want to find the baste; your heels are just a-spurrin' one another a foot below his belly!"

We were delighted to be again in our old quarters, where we were more in the world and guard duty lighter. Several times before leaving this camp our mess had visits from the two cousins, Lewis and William Randolph, the first-named a captain in the Irish Battalion, the second a captain in the Second Virginia Regiment, who stopped over-night with us, on scouting expeditions across the Rappahannock in the enemy's lines, where Willie Randolph had a sweetheart, whom he, soon after this, married. Lewis Randolph told us that he had killed a Federal soldier with a stone in the charge on the railroad-cut at second Manassas; that the man, who was about twenty steps from him, was recapping his gun, which had just missed fire while aimed at Randolph's orderly-sergeant, when he threw the stone. William Randolph said, "Yes, that's true; when we were provost-officers at Frederick, Maryland, a man was brought in under arrest and, looking at Lewis, said, 'I've seen you before. I saw you kill a Yankee at second Manassas with a stone,' and then related the circumstances exactly."

William Randolph was six feet two inches in height, and said that he had often been asked how he escaped in battle, and his reply was, "By taking a judicious advantage of the shrubbery." This, however, did not continue to avail him, as he was afterward killed while in command of his regiment, being one of the six commanders which the Second

Virginia Regiment lost—killed in battle—during the war.

In March we moved from our winter-quarters to Hamilton's Crossing, three miles from Fredericksburg, where we remained in camp, with several interruptions, until May. Our fare here was greatly improved by the addition of fresh fish, so abundant at that season of the year in the Rappahannock and the adjacent creeks. To a mountaineer familiar with the habits of the wary trout and other fish that are caught with hook and line, the manner of fishing here was very novel. Of the herring and shad left by the hundreds in the grass and shallows as the tide receded, the soldiers had only to wade in and with stick or bare hand to secure all they could carry. Circling overhead was a concourse of fish-hawks and eagles, each watching his chance to swoop down on his prey, then ascending with his catch, whose silvery sides gleamed in the sunlight like a polished bayonet, run the gauntlet of his pursuers. In April the great cavalry battle at Kelly's Ford, forty miles above, was fought, in which the "Gallant Pelham" was killed.

CHAPTER XX

THE battle at Kelly's Ford was the forerunner of
the crossing of Hooker's army to our side of the
river, although this was delayed longer than was
expected. "Fighting Joe Hooker" having succeeded
Burnside as commander of the Army of the Potomac, numbering 130,000, was the fourth Federal
general delegated to crush Lee, with less than
50,000, Longstreet's corps being still on the Virginia
peninsula. In the latter part of April we were
roused one morning before dawn to go into position on the fatal hill in the bend of the railroad.
The various divisions of the army were already in
motion from their winter-quarters, and, as they
reached the neighborhood, were deployed in line of
battle above and below.

The high hills sloping toward the river on the
enemy's side were manned with heavy siege-guns,
from which shells were thrown at intervals as our
troops came into view. Here we lay for a day or
more, with guns unlimbered, awaiting the tedious
disposition the various divisions. The bluff on

which our guns were posted, commanding, as it did,
an extensive view of the country, attracted many of
the officers, who had preceded their men, and, with
field-glasses, scanned the surroundings. I saw at
one time, within a few rods of where we stood,
Generals Lee, Jackson, D. H. and A. P. Hill, Early,
Rodes and Colston, besides a score of brigadiers.
At this time the enemy were moving across their
pontoon bridges and extending their skirmish-lines
on the right and left.

The only time I met General Jackson to speak to
him since he had left Lexington was when he rode
away from this group of officers. As I held aside
the limb of a tree in his way, near our gun, he extended his hand and, as he gave me a hearty shake,
said, "How do you do, Edward?" A short time
after this, our battery had orders to fire a few
rounds, as a sort of "feeler," and the enemy at once
replied. The officers, not having been informed of
the order, were for a time exposed to an unneces-
sary and what might have proved very serious danger. However, they withdrew before any damage
was done, although a large piece of shell which
flew past our gun gave General Colston a close call
as he tarried near it. After threatening weather,
the sun rose clear on the following morning. A
light mist which lay along the river soon disappeared, and again, as at Harper's Ferry, our elevated position afforded a superb view. A level plain
extended to the river in our front and for some

miles to the right, and as far as Fredericksburg (two miles) to the left, and beyond the river the Stafford Heights.

While we were standing admiring the scene, three horses without riders came dashing from within the Federal lines, and swept at full speed between the two armies. They ran as if on a regular race-track and conscious of the many spectators who cheered them to their best. Then, veering in their course from side to side, they finally shot through an opening made to receive them into our lines, which raised a "rebel yell," as if Jackson were passing by. One of these horses trotted into our battery and was caught and ridden by Sergeant Strickler, under the name of "Sedgwick," to the close of the war.

Hooker's crossing the river at Fredericksburg was only a feint, as the mass of his army crossed near Chancellorsville, and thither our army went, leaving Early's division, two other brigades and several batteries, including ours, to oppose Sedgwick's corps. After three days here, with occasional artillery duels, Sedgwick recrossed the river, and Early, supposing he would join Hooker, set out with his command toward Chancellorsville. Before we had gone three miles I heard General Barksdale, as he rode along the column, ask for General Early, who was a short distance ahead, and announce, "My young men have told me that the Federals are recrossing the river." A few moments later, as the two rode back together, General Early said, "If that is the case, I must go back or they will get my wagon-train."

We at once countermarched, and by eleven o'clock were back in position on the same bluff. The fourth detachment was in front and failed to get the order to countermarch, and so kept on almost to Chancellorsville, and did not rejoin us until eight o'clock the next morning (Sunday), having spent the whole night marching.

I will mention here a striking instance of what I suppose could be called the "irony of fate." My bedfellow, Stuart, as already stated, had been fearfully wounded at Winchester, his first battle. After his return many months later, he often expressed the greatest desire to pass through one battle unhurt, and regarded his companions who had done so as fortunate heroes. It was now Sunday morning and there had been heavy firing for an hour or two about Fredericksburg, and thither the third and fourth pieces were ordered. As they were starting off, I saw Stuart bidding good-by to several friends, and I, not wishing to undergo a thing so suggestive, was quietly moving off. But he called out, "Where is my partner?" and came to me, looking so jaded after his long night-march that his farewell made me rather serious. In half an hour he was dead. As he was going with his gun into position a case-shot exploded close to him and three balls passed through his body, any one of which would have been fatal.

Two other members of the battery, Henry Foutz

and J. S. Agnor, were also killed in this engagement. The position was a trying one. Two batteries had already suffered severely while occupying it, and the cannoneers of a third battery were lying inactive by their guns as ours came into it. But in less than an hour thereafter the enemy's guns were outmatched; at any rate, ceased firing. General Hoke, who had witnessed the whole affair, came and asked Major Latimer to introduce him to Captain Graham, saying he wanted to know the man whose guns could do such execution. About noon my section joined the others a short distance in rear of this place on the hills overlooking Fredericksburg.

Soon after we had gotten together, the bodies of our dead comrades were brought from the places at which they had fallen, and William Bolling, Berkeley Minor and myself, messmates of Stuart, were detailed to bury him. His body was taken in our battery ambulance, which we accompanied, to the Marye family cemetery near our old camp, and permission gotten to bury it there. If I was ever utterly miserable, it was on this Sunday afternoon as we stood, after we had dug the grave, in this quiet place, surrounded by a dense hedge of cedar, the ground and tombstones overgrown with moss and ivy, and a stillness as deep as if no war existed. Just at this time there came timidly through the hedge, like an apparition, the figure of a woman. She proved to be Mrs. Marye; and, during the battle, which had now continued four days, she had been seeking shelter from the enemy's shells in the cellar of her house. She had come to get a lock of Stuart's hair for his mother, and her presence, now added to that of our ambulance driver, as Minor read the Episcopal burial service, made the occasion painfully solemn. In less than an hour we were again with the battery and in line of battle with the whole of our battalion, twenty guns, all of which opened simultaneously on what appeared to be a column of artillery moving through the woods in our front. However, it proved to be a train of wagons, some of which were overturned and secured by us the next day.

Here we lay during the night with guns unlimbered near Gen. "Extra Billy" Smith's brigade of infantry. Next afternoon we had a fine view of a charge by Early's division, with Brigadier-Generals Gordon and Hoke riding to and fro along their lines and the division driving the Federals from their position along the crest of the hill. The greater portion of the enemy's killed and wounded were left in our hands. Many of the latter with whom we talked were heartily sick of the war and longed for the expiration of their term of service. This series of battles, continuing, as it did, at intervals for a week, was not yet done with.

After dark our battery was ordered to move down toward Fredericksburg and occupy some earthworks just outside of the town. We had been well in range of the siege-guns already, but now the only hope was that they would overshoot us. As I was on guard that night I had ample time, while pacing the breastworks, for cogitation. I heard distinctly the barking of the dogs and the clocks striking the hours during the night. When morning came, a dense fog had settled along the river, entirely concealing us, and while it hung we were ordered to pull out quietly.

Two hundred yards back from this place we came into clear sunlight and, as we turned, saw an immense balloon poised on the surface of the mist, and apparently near enough to have pierced it with a shell. Not a shot was fired at us—veiled, as we were, by the mist—until we had gotten still farther away, but then some enormous projectiles landed around us.

A question that would naturally present itself to one who had heard of the repeated victories won by the Confederate army would be, "Why were no decisive results?" By carefully studying the history of the war, the inquirer could not fail to notice that at every crisis either some flagrant failure on the part of a subordinate to execute the duty assigned to him occurred, or that some untoward accident befell the Confederate arms. Conspicuous among the latter was Jackson's fall at Chancellorsville.

That General Hooker seemed entirely ignorant of the proximity of General Lee's army was disclosed by the discovery, by General Fitz Lee, that the right flank of the Federal army was totally un-guarded.

General Jackson, when informed of this, pro-ceeded by a rapid march to throw his corps well to the right and rear of this exposed wing, and by this unexpected onset threw that portion of Hooker's army into the utmost confusion and disorder. Fall-ing night for a time checked his advance, but, while making dispositions to push the advantage gained, so as to envelope his adversary, he passed, with his staff, outside of his picket line, and when returning to re-enter was mortally wounded by his own men.

This May 4 closed the great effort of General Hooker, with 132,000 men, to "crush" General Lee's army of 47,000. The two last of the six days of his experience in the effort probably made him thankful that the loss of 20,000 of his force had been no greater.

The mortal wounding of Jackson and his death on the tenth more than offset the advantage of the victory to the Confederates. His loss was deplored by the whole army, especially by General Lee, and to his absence in later battles, conspicuously at Get-tysburg, was our failure to succeed attributed. In fact General Lee said to a friend, after the war, that with Jackson at Gettysburg our success would have been assured—a feeling that was entertained throughout the army.

On the evening of the fifth, rain, which seemed invariably to follow a great battle, fell in torrents and we went into camp drenched to the skin. After drying by a fire, I went to bed and slept for eighteen hours. Being in our old position on the hill, we converted it into a camp and there remained.

On that portion of the great plain which extended along the railroad on our right we witnessed a grand review of Jackson's old corps, now commanded by General Ewell. The three divisions, commanded, respectively, by Generals Ed. Johnson, Rodes and Early, were drawn up one behind the other, with a space of seventy-five yards between, and General Lee, mounted on "Traveler" and attended by a full staff and numerous generals, at a sweeping gallop, made first a circuit of the entire corps, then in front and rear of each division. One by one his attendants dropped out of the cavalcade. Gen. Ed. Johnson escaped a fall from his horse by being caught by one of his staff. Early soon pulled out, followed at intervals by others; but the tireless gray, as with superb ease and even strides he swept back and forth, making the turns as his rider's body inclined to right or left, absorbed attention. The distance covered was nine miles, at the end of which General Lee drew rein with only one of his staff and Gen. A. P. Hill at his side. Such spectacles were to us extremely rare, and this one was especially well timed, affording the troops, as it did, an opportunity to see that they were still formidable in number, and although Jackson was dead that the soul of the army had not passed away.

CHAPTER XXI

OPENING OF CAMPAIGN OF 1863—CROSSING TO THE
VALLEY—BATTLE AT WINCHESTER WITH MIL-
ROY—CROSSING THE POTOMAC

THE indications of another campaign were now
not wanting, but what shape it would take caused
curious speculation; that is, among those whose duty
was only to execute. Longstreet had been recalled
from the Virginia Peninsula; Hooker's hosts again
lined the Stafford Heights across the Rappahannock. At evening we listened to the music of their
bands, at night could see the glow of their camp-
fires for miles around. On June 2, Ewell's corps
first broke camp, followed in a day or two by Longstreet's while A. P. Hill's remained at Fredericksburg to observe the movements of Hooker. On the
eighth we reached Culpeper, where we remained
during the ninth, awaiting the result of the greatest
and most stubbornly contested cavalry engagement
of the war, which continued throughout the day in
our hearing—at Brandy Station. The Federals
having been driven across the river, our march was
resumed on the tenth.

On the following day we heard, at first indistinctly, toward the front of the column continued
cheering. Following on, it grew louder and louder.
We reached the foot of a long ascent, from the sum-

mit of which the shout went up, but were at a loss to know what called it forth. Arriving there, there loomed up before us the old Blue Ridge, and we, too, joined in the chorus. Moving on with renewed life, the continued greeting of those following was heard as eye after eye took in its familiar face. We had thought that the love for these old mountains was peculiar to us who had grown up among them; but the cheer of the Creoles who had been with us under Jackson was as hearty as our own.

We passed through Little Washington, thence by Chester Gap to Front Royal, the first of our old battlegrounds in the Valley, having left Longstreet's and Hill's corps on the east side of the mountain. At Winchester, as usual, was a force of the enemy under our former acquaintance, General Milroy. Without interruption we were soon in his vicinity. Nearly two days were consumed in feeling his strength and position. Our battery was posted on a commanding hill north of the town, the top of which was already furrowed with solid shot and shells to familiarize the enemy with its range. Our battery now consisted of two twenty-pound Parrott, and two brand-new English Blakeley guns, to one of which I belonged. And a singular coincidence it was that in putting in the first charge my gun was choked, the same thing having occurred on the same field a year before, being the only times it happened during the war. I went immediately to the third piece and took the place of No. 1.

The battle had now begun, the enemy firing at us from a strongly fortified fort near the town. Their target practice was no criterion of their shooting when being shot at, as not one of us was even wounded. While the battle was in progress we had a repetition of the race at Fredericksburg when there dashed from the Federal fort three artillery horses, which came at full speed over the mile between us, appearing and disappearing from view. On reaching the battery they were caught, and one of them, which we named "Milroy," was driven by James Lewis at the wheel of my gun, and restored with "Sedgwick" to his old associates at Appomattox.

Night put a stop to hostilities, and the next day, until late in the afternoon, we passed inactively. Then Hayes's Louisiana Brigade, formerly commanded by Gen. Dick Taylor, formed in our front and, charging with the old yell, captured the fort. After night I found two members of our company in possession of a little mule, equipped with saddle and bridle, supposed to be a United States animal. They said they were afraid of mules, and turned him over to me. I forthwith mounted, and passed an hour pleasantly, riding around. As I once heard a little negro say, "I went everywhar I knowed, an' everywhar I didn't know I come back." I felt now that I had a mount for the campaign, but next morning one of the Richmond Howitzers claimed the mule and identified it as his.

The bulk of Milroy's force escaped during the night, but we captured four thousand prisoners, twenty-eight pieces of artillery, and hundreds of wagons and horses, and equipped ourselves, as we had done in 1862, at the expense of Banks. For our two recently acquired English Blakeley guns we substituted two twenty-pound Parrotts, giving us four guns of the same caliber. On the thirteenth we crossed the Potomac at Sheperdstown, thence by way of Hagerstown, Maryland, to Greencastle, Pennsylvania, the first live Yankee town we had visited in war times. Many of the stores were open and full of goods, but as they refused to take Confederate money, and we were forbidden to plunder, we passed on, feeling aggrieved, and went into camp a few miles beyond.

Having a curiosity to test the resources and hospitality of this abundant country, I set out from camp, with two companions, for this purpose. A walk of a mile brought us to the house of a widow with three pretty daughters. They told us they had been feeding many of our soldiers and could give us only some milk, which they served, as seemed to be the custom of the country, in large bowls. They said they did not dislike rebels, and if we would go on to Washington and kill Lincoln, and end the war, they would rejoice. Proceeding farther, we stopped at a substantial brick house and were silently ushered into a large room, in the far end of which sat the head of the house, in clean white shirt-sleeves but otherwise dressed for company, his hat on and his feet as high as his head against the wall, smoking a cigar. At the other end of the room the rest of the family were at supper, of which we were perfunctorily asked by the mistress to partake. A very aged lady, at a corner of the table, without speaking or raising her eyes, chewed apparently the same mouthful during our stay—one of our party suggested, "perhaps her tongue." The table was thickly covered with saucers of preserves, pickles, radishes, onions, cheese, etc. The man of the house did not turn his head nor speak a word during our stay, which was naturally over with the meal.

We returned to the battalion about sunset, encamped in a clean, grassy enclosure, the horses enjoying their bountiful food, the men in gay spirits, and the regimental bands playing lively airs. Shortly after our return, there occurred an incident which lent additional interest to the occasion.

No one at all familiar with the Rockbridge Artillery will fail to remember Merrick. A lawyer and native of Hagerstown, Maryland, having been educated abroad, he was an accomplished scholar and a fine musician, with a stock of Irish and other songs which he sang admirably. In person he was very slender, over six feet in height, with a long neck, prominent nose, and very thin hair and whiskers. Cut off from home and being utterly improvident, he was entirely dependent on quartermaster's goods for his apparel, and when clothing was issued his forlorn and ragged appearance hushed every claim by others who might have had precedence. This Confederate clothing, like the rations, was very short, so that Merrick's pantaloons and jacket failed to meet, by several inches, the intervening space showing a very soiled cotton shirt. With the garments mentioned—a gray cap, rusty shoes and socks, and, in winter, half the tail of his overcoat burnt off—his costume is described.

Indifference to his appearance extended also to danger, and when a battle was on hand so was Merrick. Before crossing the Potomac he disappeared from the command a perfect-looking vagabond, and now as we were reveling in this bountiful country there rolled into our midst a handsome equipage drawn by two stylish horses. When the door was opened out stepped Merrick, handsomely dressed in citizen's clothes, and handed out two distinguished-looking gentlemen, to whom he introduced us. Then, in the language of Dick Swiveler, "he passed around the rosy"; and all taking a pull, our enthusiasm for Merrick mounted high.

Our march under Ewell had been admirably conducted. We were always on the road at an early hour, and, without hurry or the usual halts caused by troops crowding on one another, we made good distances each day and were in camp by sunset. I never before or afterward saw the men so buoyant. There was no demonstration, but a quiet undercur-

B. C. M. FRIEND

rent of confidence that they were there to conquer. The horses, too, invigorated by abundant food, carried higher heads and pulled with firmer tread.

Our march from Greencastle was through Chambersburg and Shippensburg, and when within eight or ten miles of Carlisle we passed through one or two hundred Pennsylvania militia in new Federal uniforms, who had just been captured and paroled. Before reaching Carlisle we very unexpectedly (to us) countermarched, and found the militiamen at the same place, but almost all of them barefooted, their shoes and stockings having been appropriated by needy rebels. As we first saw them they were greatly crestfallen, but after losing their footgear all spirit seemed to have gone out of them. They lingered, it may be, in anticipation of the greetings when met by wives and little ones at home, after having sallied forth so valiantly in their defense. How embarrassing bare feet would be instead of the expected trophies of war! Imagine a young fellow, too, meeting his sweetheart! That they kept each other company to the last moment, managed to reach home after night, and ate between meals for some days, we may be sure.

Before reaching Chambersburg we took a road to the left, in the direction of Gettysburg. To give an idea of the change in our diet since leaving Dixie, I give the bill-of-fare of a breakfast my mess enjoyed while on this road: Real coffee and sugar, light bread, biscuits with lard in them, butter, apple-butter, a fine dish of fried chicken, and a quarter of roast lamb!

On the morning of July 1 we passed through a division of Longstreet's corps bivouacked in a piece of woods. Our road lay across a high range of hills, from beyond which the sound of cannonading greeted us. By three o'clock that afternoon, when we reached the summit of the hills, the firing ahead had developed into the roar of a battle, and we pushed forward on the down-grade. The valley below, through which we passed, was thickly settled, and soon we began to meet prisoners and wounded, whose numbers rapidly increased as we advanced, and at the same pump by the roadside we frequently saw a group of Federal and Confederate soldiers having their wounds bathed and dressed by Northern women, kind alike to friend and foe. When we reached the field, about sundown, the battle was over. This was July 1 and the first of the three days of terrific fighting which constituted the battle of Gettysburg.

CHAPTER XXII

BEFORE proceeding farther let us consider briefly the condition of the two armies, and which had the better grounds to hope for success in the great conflict now impending. With the exception of one—Sharpsburg—which was a drawn battle, the Confederates had been victorious in every general engagement up to this time. Scant rations, deprivation, and hardships of every kind had made them tired of the war; and the recent abundance had not only put them in better fighting condition than ever before, but made them long to enjoy it permanently at home.

The Federal army had changed commanders after every defeat, and the present one—General Meade—who had just been appointed, was not an officer to inspire special confidence. With all this in favor of the Southerners, all else seemed to conspire against them. On the morning of June 30, the day before the battle, Pickett's division was at Chambersburg, thirty miles from Gettysburg; Hood's and McLaw's (the other two divisions of Longstreet's corps) fifteen miles nearer Gettysburg; Hill's corps at Cashtown, nine miles from Gettysburg; Rodes's division of Ewell's corps at Carlisle, thirty miles distant; Johnson's at Greenville, and Early's near York. General Early levied for and obtained from the city of York several thousand pairs of shoes and socks and a less number of hats for his men, and $26,000 in money.

The different portions of the Federal army at this time were spread out over a large area, south and east of Gettysburg. To the absence of our cavalry, whose whereabouts since crossing the Potomac had not been known by General Lee, was due the ignorance as to the location of the Federals, causing loss of time and the employment of other troops to do what the cavalry should have done. It is generally conceded that until they found themselves face to face the commander of neither army expected or desired this locality to be the battle-ground. And when we consider the fact that armies have been known to maneuver for weeks for a vantage ground on which to give battle, we can realize the importance of this seeming accident, which sealed the doom of the Confederacy. For if the whole State of Pennsylvania had been gone over, it is probable that no other place could have been found which afforded such advantages as did this to the Northern army.

Early's division had passed it several days before on his way to York, and Pettigrew's brigade of Hill's corps on July 1, while approaching in search of shoes for his men, encountered Buford's Federal cavalry, precipitating the first day's conflict, in which Hill's corps, Rodes's and Early's divisions captured

5,000 prisoners and drove the Federals through the town to the heights beyond.   Our battalion of artillery, soon after dark, passed southward through the outskirts of the town with Early's division and bivouacked for the night.   By dawn of the following day (July 2) sufficient of the Federal army had arrived to occupy and fortify the heights.   From where our battery was posted, a mile east of the town, we had in full view the end of Cemetery Hill, with an arched gateway for an entrance.   To the left of it and joined by a depressed ridge was Culp's Hill, steep and rugged as a mountain, all now held and fortified by the enemy.   Jackson's old division, now commanded by Gen. Ed. Johnson, having arrived late in the night, formed at the base of Culp's Hill, and before an hour of daylight had elapsed had stirred up a hornets' nest in their front.

I must mention an incident that occurred during this forenoon quite interesting to myself.   As we were standing by our guns, not yet having fired a shot, General Ewell and his staff came riding by, and Lieut.-Col. Sandy Pendleton, his adjutant, rode out from among them and handed me two letters. To receive two letters in the army at any time was an event, but here, away in the enemy's country, in the face of their frowning guns, for them to have come so far and then be delivered at the hands of the General and his staff was quite something.   One of the letters I recognized as being from my mother, the other aroused my curiosity.   The envelope, di-

rected in a feminine hand, was very neat, but the
end had been burned off and the contents were held
in place by a narrow red ribbon daintily tied. In
so conspicuous a place, with a battle on, I could not
trust myself to open my treasures. It was near
night before a suitable time came, and my billet-doux
contained the following:

> *You are cordially invited to be present*
> *at the Commencement Exercises of the*
> *—— Female Seminary, on the evening*
> *of July 3rd, 1863, at eight o'clock* P. M.
> *Compliments of Gertrude ——.*

My feelings were inexpressible. How I longed
to be there! To think of such a place of quiet and
peace as compared with my surroundings on this
bloody battlefield!

But to return to the serious features of the day.
With the exception of the steady musketry firing
by Johnson's men on Culp's Hill, the day passed
quietly until nearly four o'clock. At this time Andrew's battalion of artillery, led by Major Latimer,
passed in front of us and went into position two
hundred yards to our left, and nearer the enemy.
The ground sloped so as to give us a perfect view of
his four batteries. Promptly other batteries joined
those confronting us on Cemetery Hill, and by the
time Latimer's guns were unlimbered the guns on
both sides were thundering.

In less than five minutes one of Latimer's caissons was exploded, which called forth a lusty cheer from the enemy. In five minutes more a Federal caisson was blown up, which brought forth a louder cheer from us. In this action Latimer's batteries suffered fearfully, the Alleghany Roughs alone losing twenty-seven men killed and wounded. Only one or two were wounded in our battery, the proximity of Latimer's guns drawing the fire to them. Near the close of the engagement, Latimer, who was a graduate of the Virginia Military Institute, a mere youth in appearance, was killed.

The artillery contest was a small part of the afternoon's work. One of Johnson's brigades, after capturing breastworks and prisoners on Culp's Hill, pushed nearly to General Meade's headquarters. Rodes, usually so prompt, was occupying the town and failed to attack till late, and then with but two of his four brigades; but they charged over three lines of breastworks and captured several pieces of artillery, which had to be abandoned for want of support. Sickles's corps, having occupied the two "Round Tops" on the extreme left of the Federal line, advanced on Longstreet, and at four P. M. the two lines met in the celebrated "Peach Orchard," and from that time until night fought furiously, the Federals being driven back to their original ground.

At the close of the second day the Confederates had gained ground on the right and left, and captured some artillery, but still nothing decisive. An-

other night passed, and the third and last day
dawned on two anxious armies.   Pickett, after a
mysterious delay of twenty-four hours, arrived during the forenoon and became the left of Longstreet's
corps.   At twelve o'clock word was passed along our
lines that when two signal-guns were heard, followed by heavy firing, to open vigorously with our
guns.   There was no mistaking when that time came,
and we joined with the three hundred guns that
made the firing.   For an hour or more a crash and
roar of artillery continued that rolled and reverberated above, and made the earth under us tremble.
When it began there was great commotion among
the enemy's batteries in our front, some of which
limbered up and galloped along the crest of Cemetery Hill, but soon returned and renewed their fire
on us.

So far they had failed to do our battery any
serious harm, but now each volley of their shells
came closer and closer.   At this time my attention
was attracted to the second piece, a few paces to our
left, and I saw a shell plow into the ground under
Lieutenant Brown's feet and explode.   It tore a
large hole, into which Brown sank, enveloped as he
fell in smoke and dust.   In an instant another shell
burst at the trail of my gun, tearing the front half
of Tom Williamson's shoe off, and wounding him
sorely.   A piece of it also broke James Ford's leg,
besides cutting off the fore leg of Captain Graham's
horse.   Ford was holding the lead-horses of the

limber, and, as they wheeled to run, their bridles were seized by Rader, a shell struck the horse nearest to him, and, exploding at the instant, killed all four of the lead-horses and stunned Rader. These same horses and this driver had very nearly a similar experience (though not so fatal) at Sharpsburg a year before, as already described. Sam Wilson, another member of our detachment, was also painfully wounded and knocked down by the same shell.

This artillery bombardment was the prelude to Pickett's charge, which took place on the opposite side of Cemetery Hill, and out of our view. Culp's Hill, since the early morning previous, had been enveloped in a veil of smoke from Johnson's muskets, which had scarcely had time to cool during the thirty-six hours.

The men of the Fourth Virginia Regiment had been gradually and steadily advancing from boulder to boulder, until they were almost under the enemy's fortifications along the crest of the ridge. To proceed farther was physically impossible, to retreat was almost certain death. So, of the College company alone, one of whom had already been killed and many wounded, sixteen, including Captain Strickler, were captured. To John McKee, of this company, a stalwart Irish Federal said as he reached out to pull him up over the breastworks, "Gim-me your hand, Johnny Reb; you've give' us the bulliest fight of the war!"

Lieutenant "Cush" Jones determined to run the

gauntlet for escape, and as he darted away the
point of his scabbard struck a stone, and throwing
it inverted above his head, lost out his handsome
sword. Three bullets passed through his clothing in
his flight, and the boulder behind which he next took
refuge was peppered by others. Here, also, my
former messmate, George Bedinger, now captain of
a company in the Thirty-third Virginia Regiment,
was killed, leading his "Greeks," as he called his
men.

About nine o'clock that evening, and before we
had moved from our position, I received a message,
through Captain Graham, from some of the wounded
of our company, to go to them at their field-hospital.
Following the messenger, I found them in charge of
our surgeon, Dr. Herndon, occupying a neat brick
cottage a mile in the rear, from which the owners
had fled, leaving a well-stocked larder, and from it
we refreshed ourselves most gratefully.   Toward
midnight orders came to move. The ambulances
were driven to the door and, after the wounded,
some eight or ten in number, had been assisted into
them, I added from the stores in the house a bucket
of lard, a crock of butter, a jar of apple-butter, a
ham, a middling of bacon, and a side of sole-leather.
All for the wounded!

Feeling assured that we would not tarry much
longer in Pennsylvania, and expecting to reach the
battery before my services would be needed, I set
out with the ambulances. We moved on until day-

light and joined the wounded of the other batteries of our battalion, and soon after left, at a house by the wayside, a member of the Richmond Howitzers who was dying. Our course was along a by-road in the direction of Hagerstown. In the afternoon, after joining the wagon-train, I found "Joe," the colored cook of my mess, in possession of a super-numerary battery-horse, which I appropriated and mounted. Our column now consisted of ambulances loaded with wounded men, wounded men on foot, cows, bulls, quartermasters, portable forges, sur-geons, cooks, and camp-followers in general, all plodding gloomily along through the falling rain.

We arrived at the base of the mountain about five p. m. and began ascending by a narrow road, leading obliquely to the left. Before proceeding farther some description of the horse I was riding is appropriate, as he proved an important factor in my experiences before the night was over. He was the tallest horse I ever saw outside of a show, with a very short back and exceedingly long legs, which he handled peculiarly, going several gaits at one time. Many a cannoneer had sought rest on his back on the march, but none had ventured on so high a perch when going into battle. When half-way up the mountain we heard to our left oblique the distant mutter of a cannon, then in a few mo-ments the sound was repeated, but we thought it was safely out of our course and felt correspond-ingly comfortable. At intervals the report of that gun was heard again and again. About dusk we reached the top of the mountain, after many, many halts, and the sound of that cannon became more emphatic.

After descending a few hundred yards there came from a bridle-path on our left, just as I passed it, three cavalry horses with empty saddles. This was rather ominous. The halts in the mixed column were now frequent, darkness having set in, and we had but little to say. That cannon had moved more to our front, and our road bore still more to where it was thundering. We were now almost at the foot of the mountain, and to the left, nearer our front, were scattering musket-shots. Our halts were still short and frequent, and in the deep shadow of the mountain it was pitch-dark. All of this time I had not a particle of confidence in my horse. I could not tell what was before me in the dense darkness, whether friend or foe, but suddenly, after pausing an instant, he dashed forward. For fifty or seventy-five yards every other sound was drowned by a roaring waterfall on my right; then, emerging from its noise, I was carried at a fearful rate close by dismounted men who were firing from behind trees along the roadside, the flashes of their guns, "whose speedy gleams the darkness swallowed," revealing me on my tall horse with his head up. He must see safety ahead, and I let him fly.

A hundred yards farther on our road joined the main pike at an acute angle, and entering it he swept on. Then, just behind me, a Federal cannon was discharged. The charge of canister tore through the brush on either side, and over and under me, and at the same instant my steed's hind leg gave way, and my heart sank with it. If struck at all, he immediately rallied and outran himself as well as his competitors. After getting out of the range of the firing and the shadow of the mountain, I saw indistinctly our cavalrymen along the side of the road, and we bantered each other as I passed.

Farther on, at a toll-gate, I heard the voice of Tom Williamson. His ambulance had broken down and he was being assisted toward the house. I drew rein, but thought, "How can I help him? This horse must be well-nigh done for," and rode on. Since reaching the foot of the mountain the way had been open and everything on it moving for life. But again the road was full, and approaching clatter, with the sharp reports of pistols, brought on another rush, and away we went—wagons, wounded men, negroes, forges, ambulances, cavalry—everything.

This in time subsided and, feeling ashamed, I turned back to look after my wounded, my horse as reluctant as myself, and expecting every moment the sound of the coming foe. A sudden snort and the timid step of my nervous steed warned me of breakers ahead. Peering through the darkness I saw coming toward me, noisless and swift as the wind, an object white as the driven snow. "What,"

I asked myself, "are ghosts abroad, and in such a place? Is Gettysburg giving up her dead so soon?" But, as the thing met me, a voice cried out, "It that you, Ned? Is that you? Take me on your horse. Let me get in the saddle and you behind." For a moment I was dumb, and wished it wasn't I. The voice was the voice of Lieutenant Brown, the same whom I had seen undermined by the shell at Gettysburg, and who had not put a foot to the ground until now. Barefooted, bareheaded; nothing on but drawers and shirt—white as a shroud! The prospect that now confronted me instantly flashed through my mind. First, "Can this horse carry two?" Then I pictured myself with such a looking object in my embrace, and with nothing with which to conceal him. There were settlements ahead, daylight was approaching, and what a figure we would cut! It was too much for me, and I said, "No, get on behind," feeling that the specter might retard the pursuing foe. But my tall horse solved the difficulty. Withdrawing my foot from the stirrup, Brown would put his in and try to climb up, when suddenly the horse would "swap ends," and down he'd go. Again he would try and almost make it, and the horse not wheeling quickly enough I would give him the hint with my "off" heel. My relief can be imagined when an ambulance arrived and took Brown in. I accompanied him for a short distance, then quickened my pace and overtook the train. Presently another clatter behind and the popping of pistols. Riding at my side was a horseman, and by the flash of his pistol I saw it pointing to the ground at our horses' feet.

Reaching the foot of a hill, my horse stumbled and fell as if to rise no more. I expected to be instantly trampled out of sight. I heard a groan, but not where the horse's head should have been. Resting my feet on the ground, thus relieving him of my weight, he got his head from under him and floundered forward, then to his feet and away. Farther on, a swift horse without a rider was dashing by me. I seized what I supposed to be his bridle-rein, but it proved to be the strap on the saddle-bow, and the pull I gave came near unhorsing me.

The pursuit continued no farther. Not having slept for two days and nights, I could not keep awake, and my game old horse, now wearied out, would stagger heedlessly against the wheels of moving wagons. Just at dawn of day, in company with a few horsemen of our battalion, I rode through the quiet streets of Hagerstown, thence seven miles to Williamsport.

The wounded of our battalion had all been captured. A few, however, were not carried off, but left until our army came up. Some of the cooks, etc., escaped by dodging into the brush, but many a good horse and rider had been run down and taken. At Williamsport I exchanged horses with an infantryman while he was lying asleep on a porch, and had completed the transaction before he was sufficiently awake to remonstrate.

It must not be supposed from the experience we had undergone that our army was at all demoralized. The battle closed on July 3rd. On the next day our lines began to withdraw, Ewell's corps holding its ground till near noon of the 5th. The Federal commander, though repeatedly urged by the Washington authorities to do so, declined to attack during that time. Our army was prevented from crossing the Potomac, swollen by heavy rains, till the 14th, meantime not only offering but inviting battle, which was steadily declined.

We were now entirely cut off from our army, and with what of the wagons, etc., that remained were at the mercy of the enemy, as the Potomac was swollen to a depth of twenty feet where I had waded a year before. Most of the horses had to be *swum over,* as there was little room in the ferry-boats for them. The river was so high that this was very dangerous, and only expert swimmers dared to undertake it. Twenty dollars was paid for swimming a horse over, and I saw numbers swept down by the current and landed hundreds of yards below, many on the side from which they had started. I crossed in a ferry-boat on my recently acquired horse, having left my faithful old charger, his head encased in mud to the tips of his ears, with mingled feelings of sadness and gratitude.

A great curiosity to understand this battle and battlefield induced me to visit it at the first opportunity, and in 1887, twenty-four years after it was fought, I, with Colonel Poague, gladly accepted an invitation from the survivors of Pickett's division to go with them to Gettysburg, whither they had been invited to meet the Philadelphia Brigade, as their guests, and go over the battlefield together. After our arrival there, in company with two officers of the Philadelphia Brigade, one of Pickett's men and an intelligent guide, I drove over the field. As a part of our entertainment we saw the Pickett men formed on the same ground and in the same order in which they had advanced to the charge. Farther on we saw the superb monuments, marking the location of the different Federal regiments, presenting the appearance of a vast cemetery. The position held by the Federals for defense was perfect. Its extent required the whole of the Confederate army present to occupy the one line they first adopted, with no troops to spare for flanking. Its shape, somewhat like a fish-hook, enabled the Federal army to reinforce promptly any part that was even threatened. Its terrain was such that the only ground sufficiently smooth for an enemy to advance on, that in front of its center, was exposed throughout, not only to missiles from its front, but could be raked from the heights on its left. And, in addition to all this, the whole face of the country, when the battle was fought, was closely intersected with post and rail and stone fences.

CHAPTER XXIII

AT "THE BOWER"—RETURN TO ORANGE COUNTY,
VIRGINIA—BLUE RUN CHURCH—BRISTOW STA-
TION—RAPPAHANNOCK BRIDGE—SUPPLEMENT-
ING CAMP RATIONS

To RETURN to my retreat from Gettysburg. The
clothes that I wore were all that I now possessed.
My blanket, extra wearing apparel, lard, apple-butter, sole-leather, etc., with the wounded, were in the
hands of the Federals. Being completely cut off
from our army, I set out for Winchester. Near
Martinsburg I passed the night sleeping on the
ground—my first sleep in sixty hours—and reached
Winchester the following day. In a day or two,
thinking our army had probably reached the Potomac, I turned back to join it. On my way thither
I called at "The Bower," the home of my messmate,
Steve Dandridge. This was a favorite resort of
Gen. J. E. B. Stuart, where, accompanied by the
celebrated banjoist, Joe Sweeny, merry nights were
passed with song and dance. I was overwhelmed
with kindness by Mr. and Mrs. Dandridge, their
daughters, nieces, and cousins. The last named being two Misses Conrad, of Martinsburg, whose two
brothers, Tucker and Holmes, had been killed at the
same instant at first Manassas, and fell clasped in

each other's arms. They would not hear of my leaving; at any rate, until they had time to make me some undergarments. In the afternoon I accompanied the young ladies to the fields blackberrying, and had some jolly laughs. They felt that a Confederate soldier should be treated like a king, that he must be worn out with marching and fighting. They insisted on my sitting in the shade while they gathered and brought me the choicest berries, and actually wanted to let the fences down, to save me the effort of climbing. At that time I weighed one hundred and ninety pounds, was in vigorous health and strength, tough as hickory, and could go over or through a Virginia rail fence as deftly as a mule. It was some days before our army could recross the Potomac, on account of high water. As I rode in, on my return to the battery, I was given a regular cheer, all thinking that I was probably, by that time, in Fort Delaware.

Our wounded had been captured in Pennsylvania, except Tom Williamson, who was left at the toll-house and picked up as our battery came by. As he had become my bedfellow since Stuart's death, I was sent with him to Winchester, where I cared for him at the home of Mrs. Anne Magill. During my stay Randolph Tucker, a brother of Mrs. Magill, and Bishop Wilmer, of Alabama, were guests in the house, and Mr. Tucker kept the household alive with his songs and jokes. After a week or more in camp, near Bunker Hill, our despondent army passed through Winchester, thence by Front Royal across

the Blue Ridge, and encamped for the remainder of
the summer in Orange County, with men and horses
greatly depleted in number and spirits.

Our battery camped at Blue Run Church and near
a field of corn. Roasting ears afforded the chief
portion of our living. It was surprising to see how
much, in addition to the army rations, a man could
consume day after day, or rather night after night,
with no especial alteration in his physique.

Soup was a favorite dish, requiring, as it did, but
one vessel for all the courses, and the more ingredients it contained, the more it was relished. Merrick claimed to be an adept in the culinary art, and
proposed to several of us that if we would "club in"
with him he would concoct a pot that would be food
for the gods. He was to remain in camp, have the
water boiling, and the meat sufficiently cooked by
the time the others returned from their various
rounds in search of provender. In due time, one
after another, the foragers showed up, having been
very successful in their acquisitions, which, accord-
ing to Merrick's directions, were consigned to the
pot. As some fresh contribution, which he regarded
as especially savory, was added, Merrick's countenance would brighten up. At one time he sat quietly
musing, then gave expression to his joy in an Irish
ditty. His handsome suit of clothes, donned at
Hagerstown, was now in tatters, which made his
appearance the more ludicrous as he "cut the pigeon-
wing" around the seething cauldron. He had par-

JOHN M. BROWN
(War-time portrait)

ticularly enjoined upon us, when starting out, to procure, at all hazards, some okra, which we failed to get, and, in naming aloud the various items, as each appeared on the surface of the water, he wound up his soliloquy with, "And now, Lord, for a little okra!"

In September the army moved again toward Manassas, about seventy miles distant. When we arrived at Bristow, the next station south of Manassas, an engagement had just taken place, in which Gen. A. P. Hill had been disastrously outwitted by his adversary, General Warren, and the ground was still strewn with our dead. The Federals were drawn up in two lines of battle, the one in front being concealed in the railroad-cut, while the rear line, with skirmishers in front, stood in full view. The Confederates, unaware of the line in the cut, advanced to the attack without skirmishers and were terribly cut up by the front line, and driven back, with a loss of several pieces of artillery and scores of men. The delay caused by this unfortunate affair gave the Federal army ample time to withdraw at leisure. General Lee arrived on the scene just at the close of this affair and was asked, by General Hill, if he should pursue the then retreating Federals. He replied, "No, General Hill; all that can now be done is to bury your unfortunate dead."

After this we returned to the west side of the Rappahannock and encamped at Pisgah Church, overlooking the plains about Brandy Station. As the war was prolonged, Confederate rations proportionately diminished, both in quantity and variety. Consequently, to escape the pangs of hunger, the few opportunities that presented themselves were gladly seized. In the absence of the sportsmen of peace times, game had become quite abundant, especially quail. But our "murmurings," if any there were, did not avail, as did those of the Israelites, "to fill the camp." I soon succeeded in getting an Enfield rifle, a gun not designed for such small game. By beating Minie-balls out flat, then cutting the plates into square blocks or slugs, I prepared my ammunition, and in the first eleven shots killed nine quail on the wing. I was shooting for the pot, and shot to kill.

From this camp our battery was ordered to occupy a fort on the west side of the river, near Rappahannock Station. Immediately across the river Hayes's and Hoke's brigades of Early's division occupied a line of breastworks as a picket or outpost. A pontoon bridge (a bridge of boats), in place of the railroad bridge, which had been burned, served as a crossing. While a dozen or more of our battery were a mile in the rear of the fort, getting a supply of firewood, another member of the company came to us at a gallop, with orders to return as quickly as possible to the fort. On our arrival the indications of an attack from the enemy were very apparent. They must have anticipated immense slaughter, as no less than a hundred of their ambulances were plainly visible. About four P. M. they opened on us with artillery, and from that time until sundown a spirited contest was kept up. While this was in progress their infantry advanced, but, after a brief but rapid fire of musketry, almost perfect quiet was restored.

While working at my gun I received what I thought to be a violent kick on the calf of my leg, but, turning to discover whence the blow came, saw a Minie-ball spinning on the ground. It was very painful for a time, but did not interrupt my service at the gun. It was too dark for us to see what was going on across the river, but the sudden and complete stillness following the firing was very mysterious. While speculating among ourselves as to what it meant, a half-naked infantryman came almost breathless into our midst and announced that both brigades had been captured, he having escaped by swimming the river. One of our lieutenants refused to believe his statement and did the worthy fellow cruel injustice in accusing him of skulking. That his story was true soon became evident. Our situation was now extremely dangerous, as the Federals had only to cross on the pontoon bridge a hundred yards from the fort and "gobble us up." About nine o'clock General Early, with his other two brigades, arrived. After acquainting himself with the surrounding conditions, he asked our batterymen for a volunteer to burn the bridge. To accomplish this would involve extreme danger, as the moment a light was struck for the purpose a hundred shots could be expected from the opposite end, not more than seventy-five yards away. However, William Effinger, of Harrisonburg, Virginia, one of our cannoneers, promptly volunteered to undertake it; and soon had the bridge in flames, the enemy not firing a shot. For this gallant and daring act, Effinger, after a long time, received a lieutenant's commission and was assigned to another branch of the service.

From this perilous situation we came off surprisingly well, but lost Robert Bell, of Winchester, Virginia. He was struck by a large piece of shell, which passed through his body. During the hour he survived, his companions who could leave their posts went to say good-by. He was a brave soldier and a modest, unassuming gentleman as well. The Federals, satisfied with the capture of the two celebrated brigades without loss to themselves, withdrew—and again we returned to the vicinity of Brandy Station.

In an artillery company two sentinels are kept on post—one to see after the guns and ammunition, the other to catch and tie loose horses or extricate them when tangled in their halters, and the like. Merrick's name and mine, being together on the roll, we were frequently on guard at the same time, and, to while away the tedious hours of the night, would seek each other's company. Our turn came while in this camp one dark, chilly night; the rain falling fast and the wind moaning through the leafless woods.

As we stood near a fitful fire, Merrick, apparently becoming oblivious of the dismal surroundings, began to sing. He played the rôle of a lover serenading his sweetheart, opening with some lively air to attract her attention. The pattering of the rain he construed as her tread to the lattice; then poured forth his soul in deepest pathos, "Hear me, Norma, in pity hear me!" (the progress of his suit being interpreted, aside, to me), and again fixed his gaze on the imaginary window. Each sound made by the storm he explained as some recognition; the creaking of a bent tree was the gentle opening of the casement, and the timely falling of a bough broken by the wind was a bouquet thrown to his eager grasp, over which he went into raptures. Whether the inspiration was due to a taste of some stimulant or to his recurring moods of intense imagination, I could not say, but the performance was genuinely artistic.

During the last night of our sojourn in this camp I had another experience of as fully absorbing interest. A very tough piece of beef (instead of quail) for supper proved more than my digestive organs could stand. After retiring to my bunk several sleepless hours passed wrestling with my burden. About one o'clock, the struggle being over, with an intense feeling of comfort I was falling into a sound sleep when I heard, in the distance, the shrill note of a bugle, then another and another, as camp after camp was invaded by urgent couriers; then our own bugle took up the alarm and sounded the call to hitch up. Meantime, drums were rolling, till the hitherto stillness of night had become a din of noise. We packed up and pulled out through the woods in the dark, with gun No. 1, to which I belonged, the rear one of the battery. A small bridge, spanning a ditch about five feet deep, had been passed over safely by the other guns and caissons in front, but when my gun-carriage was midway on it the whole structure collapsed. The struggle the detachment of men and horses underwent during the rest of this night of travail constituted still another feature of the vicissitudes of "merry war." Fortunately for us, Lieut. Jack Jordan was in charge, and, as Rockbridge men can testify, any physical difficulty that could not be successfully overcome by a Jordan, where men and horses were involved, might well be despaired of.

After reaching the Rapidan, a day was spent skirmishing with the enemy's artillery on the hills beyond. After which both sides withdrew—we to our former camps.

A short time thereafter I called on my old friends of the College company, whom we seldom met since our severance from the Stonewall Brigade. Two of these college boys, Tedford Barclay and George Chapin, told me that a recent provision had been announced, to the effect that a commission would be granted to any private who should perform some act of conspicuous gallantry in battle, and they had each resolved to earn the offered reward, and to be privates no longer. They were tired of carrying muskets and cartridge-boxes; and, in the next fight, as they expressed it, they had determined to be "distinguished or extinguished."

The determined manner with which it was said impressed me, so that I awaited results with interest. A fortnight had not elapsed before their opportunity came, and they proved true to their resolve. Under a galling fire their regiment hesitated to advance, when the two lads pushed to the front of the line of battle and climbed an intervening fence. Chapin was killed, and Barclay, who survives to this day, received for his daring courage the promised commission as lieutenant.

CHAPTER XXIV

BATTLE OF MINE RUN—MARCH TO FREDERICK'S
HALL—WINTER-QUARTERS—SOCIAL AFFAIRS—
AGAIN TO THE FRONT—NARROW ESCAPE FROM
CAPTURE BY GENERAL DAHLGREN—FURLOUGHS
—CADETS RETURN FROM NEW MARKET—SPOTT-
SYLVANIA AND THE WILDERNESS—RETURN TO
ARMY AT HANOVER JUNCTION—PANIC AT
NIGHT

THE movement in which we were next engaged
included the battle of Mine Run, which has been
designated by a military critic as "a campaign of
strategy," an account of which is, therefore, not
within my province. The Federals on this occasion
did most of the marching and, after crossing the
Rapidan at several different fords, were confronted
not far from our quarters at Mine Run, in Orange
County. After breaking camp our first intimation
that a battle was expected was the invariable pro-
fusion of playing-cards along the road. I never saw
or heard of a Bible or prayer-book being cast aside
at such a time, but cards were always thrown away
by soldiers going into battle.

After a spirited engagement between Johnson's
division and Warren's corps, the Federals lost time
sufficient for the Confederates to construct a for-

midable line of breastworks. The position occupied by our battery was in the midst of a brigade of North Carolinians who had seen some service in their own State, but had never participated in a real battle. From a Federal shell, which burst some distance overhead, a thin piece twirled downward and fell like a leaf within a few feet of our gun. I saw one of their lieutenants, who was lying in the trench, eye it suspiciously, then creep out and pick it up. Presently the colonel of his regiment passed along and the lieutenant said, as he held up the trophy, "Colonel, just look at this. I was lying right *here,* and it fell right *there.*" This brigade had no occasion to test its mettle until the following spring, but then, in the great battle of Spottsylvania, it fought gallantly and lost its general (Wright), who was killed.

Naturally, after such a determined advance on the part of the Federals, a general attack was expected; but, after spending two days threatening different portions of our lines, they withdrew in the night, leaving only men sufficient to keep their campfires burning for a time, as a ruse. The road along which we followed them for some miles was strewn at intervals with feathers from the beds of the people whose houses they had ransacked.

It was now October, and the chilly autumn nights suggested retiring to more comfortable surroundings. Our battalion of artillery was ordered to Frederick's Hall, on the Chesapeake and Ohio Railroad, about fifty miles from Richmond. In this neighborhood there were quite a number of nice people, whose society and hospitality afforded those of us so inclined much agreeable entertainment. A white paper-collar became no unusual sight, but when two of our members appeared one afternoon adorned with blue cravats a sensation was created.

A member of our battery returned from a visit to a family of former acquaintances some twelve miles from camp, and brought an invitation for some of his friends to accompany him on his next visit. Soon thereafter four of us went, through a drizzling rain, I riding a blind horse, the others on foot. Night overtook us soon after leaving camp, and when, within a mile of our destination, we asked at a house by the roadside for directions as to the way, a gruff voice informed us that an intervening creek was too high to cross, and insisted on our coming in and spending the night. We declined this, and the man said, "Well, I'll send a negro boy with you; but you'll have to come back," which proved to be the case. On our return we were boisterously welcomed. A blazing fire of dry pine soon lit up the room, with its clean, bare floor, and disclosed the figure of our host—Peter Johnson by name—a stout, burly man, clad in homespun and a fur cap. He said his wife and children had been "a-bed" since dark, were tired of his jokes, and that he was delighted to have a fresh audience; that it was past supper-time and some hours before breakfast, but that fasting was

nothing new to Confederate soldiers. The names of
two of our party, McCorkle and McClintic, he said,
were too long and that he would call them Cockle and
Flint, but before proceeding further he would give
us some music. Forthwith he produced a short flute,
took a seat on the foot of the stairs (in the far corner of the room), and played "The Devil's Dream,"
"The Arkansas Traveler," etc., beating time with
his foot.

Here we passed the night in comfortable beds and,
after a bountiful breakfast, left with a pressing invitation to return for a rabbit-chase with his hounds,
which we gladly accepted and afterward enjoyed.
This was typical of eastern Virginia and her hospitable, whole-souled "Tuckahoes," whose houses
were never too full for them to hail a passer-by and
compel him to come in. This interruption detracted
nothing from the pleasure of the visit for which we
had originally set out.

A short time after our return to Frederick's Hall
our whole artillery command narrowly escaped capture by a band of cavalry raiders under command of
Colonel Dahlgren. About fifty of the cannoneers
of the battalion had been furnished with muskets
and regularly exercised in the infantry drill. When
the raiders arrived within a mile of our winter-quarters they inquired of the country people as to the
character of troops occupying our camp, and were
informed by some negroes that the "men had muskets with bayonets on them." As infantry was not

what they were seeking, they gave us the go-by and passed on toward Richmond, the capture of which was the chief object of the expedition. In the attack on Richmond, which occurred in the night, Dahlgren was killed and his command defeated with heavy loss.

Encouraged by the visit already mentioned, I accompanied my friend, Tom Williamson, on a visit by rail to his relations, the Garnetts, near Hanover Junction; thence, after spending the night, to some friends in Caroline County. On our return to camp we found preparations on foot for a move to the front, and although we left camp by eleven o'clock that night not more than three or four miles was traveled by daylight. In the darkness one of our twenty-pounders went over a thirty-foot embankment, carrying the drivers and eight horses into the mud and water at its base.

While on the march later in the day, to save distance, I undertook to pass near a house, in the yard of which were two men with a large Newfoundland dog. A smaller dog, chained to the corner of the house, broke loose as I passed and viciously seized the tail of my overcoat. Instantly, to my dismay, the large dog left the men and dashed straight for me; but, instead of rending me, knocked my assailant heels over head and held him down until secured by the men and chained.

Before reaching the front, it was learned that we had been called out on a false alarm. Our return to

Frederick's Hall was by a more circuitous route, near which was an establishment where apple-brandy was for sale. The stock had been heavily watered and the price of shares (in a drink), even then, too far above par for eleven dollars a month to afford scarcely more than a smell. However, after reaching camp, more than ordinary wrestling and testing of strength were indulged in.

Two years had elapsed since any furloughs had been given, except to the sick and wounded. The granting of them was now revived, and those who had been longest from home were, of course, to be served first. My turn came in March. I shall never forget the impression made on me as I sat at the supper-table at home, on the evening of my arrival. My father, mother, sisters, and little niece, Bessie Nelson, were present. The last named, who had formerly treated me as scarcely an equal, now eyed me with even some degree of reverence.

After the noise, loud talking, etc., in camp, the quiet was painful. It was just as it had always been, except the vacant places of the boys at the front; still, I felt that something was wrong. Equally as impressive was the mild diet of cold bread, milk, and weak-looking tea. The effect was the same as that produced by a sudden transition from a low to a high altitude, or vice versa, requiring time for adaptation, as I soon experienced. My fifteen days' leave of absence having expired, I returned to camp.

To induce the boys who were under age, and still

at home, to enlist, a thirty-day furlough was offered to every soldier who would secure a recruit for the service. By this means many boys of only fifteen or sixteen years joined the army, to enable a long-absent kinsman to get home. McClintic, of my mess, got this furlough by the enlistment of his brother, and while at home drummed up the son of a neighbor, William Barger, whom he brought back with him to repeat the operation. To allowing this second furlough the authorities, right or wrong, objected. The matter was compromised by McClintic very generously assigning the young recruit to my credit, by which I got the furlough.

Before my return to the army, at the expiration of the thirty days, the Grant campaign had opened and the great battles of the Wilderness and Spottsylvania had been fought. Our battery had escaped without serious loss, as the character of the country afforded little opportunity for the use of artillery. From Staunton I traveled on a freight train with the cadets of the Virginia Military Institute and their professors, who were now the conspicuous heroes of the hour, having just won immortal fame in their charge, on May 15, at New Market. Among the professors was my friend and former messmate, Frank Preston, with an empty sleeve, now captain of a cadet company, and Henry A. Wise, Jr., who took command of the cadets after the wounding of Colonel Shipp, their commandant.

Our army was now near Hanover Junction, twen-

WILLIAM McCLINTIC

ty-five miles from Richmond, and engaged in its death struggle with Grant's countless legions. If any one period of the four years of the war were to be selected as an example of Southern endurance and valor, it probably should be the campaign from the Wilderness, beginning May 5 and closing a month later at Petersburg, in which the Confederate army, numbering 64,000 half-clothed, half-fed men, successfully resisted a splendidly equipped army of 140,000—inflicting a loss of 60,000 killed and wounded.

Any account or record of a war which failed to at least make mention of the events in that war which towered above all others, and which immortalized the immediate actors and shed luster on the whole army, would be incomplete. I therefore take pride in paying tribute to those men who on three separate occasions in the campaign, then in progress, displayed a species of valor and sublime conduct, *the parallel of which is recorded nowhere else in history.*

The events referred to were: First, on the morning of May 6, when our lines had been broken by the tremendous assaults of the enemy and to restore them, General Lee undertook in person to lead General Gregg's brigade of Texans in the charge. When the order to advance was given, these men, who had never before even paused to obey, now stood motionless as if some strange spell had come over them, too modest, at first, to explain the cause of their refusal, till one of their number made bold to call out, "General Lee to the rear," which was at once repeated from a hundred throats. Then yielding to the appeals of men and officers not to expose his life, the Texas brigade moved forward as one man.

Again on May 10th a similar emergency calling General Lee to the breach, two regiments, one of Georgians and one of Virginians, the Forty-ninth Virginia, refused, as did the Texans, to heed the command "Forward," until General Lee had consented to withdraw, then the line advanced.

Two such events are sufficient to establish the claim made, but as evidence that they were not the promptings of some sudden and passing impulse, two days thereafter, on May 12th, a band of Mississippians repeated the scene. Since every nation holds some particular display of fortitude and valor on the part of its soldiers, as its peculiar heritage, so we of the South should offer these exhibitions of dauntless and sublime heroism.

The English have the charge at Balaklava, the French the heroism of "The Old Guard," the Spartans their Thermopylæ, the Romans their Marcus Curtius. It required the pen of a Homer to paint the feats of valor of a Hector or an Achilles as they advanced to join in single combat amid the plaudits of admiring gods and men; the inspired language of Holy Writ to thrill us with the valor of a David in his contest with the Giant. But we are told also what there was to impel him, that when in obedience to the Divine call, he joined his people, who day after day had been cowering under the derisive taunts of their adversaries; that there was a promise from King Saul that whoever would vanquish this lusty giant would be rewarded with the hand of the king's daughter, and then to awaken all the courage he could muster he was asked in contempt by his elder brother, "With whom hast thou left those *few* sheep in the wilderness?" So when he advanced with his five smooth pebbles "from out the brook" there was nothing lacking to nerve his whole being.

Returning to our examples of valor, the surroundings of these Southerners must also be taken into account. As already stated, in every other instance in which men have displayed exalted heroism and won immortal fame, it requires but little consideration to see that none possessed the element that animated these men of the South. In some instances the others were led by some renowned chieftain, whom they felt it a credit to *follow,* as the grenadiers followed Napoleon at the Bridge of Lodi.

Others had their courage inspired and pride invoked by a contest with a single adversary, but in the case of the Southern men all of these elements were wanting. Then, too, the Northern men, whom they were now confronting, were the seasoned veterans of all the armies that had been brought against them in campaign after campaign and had proven themselves formidable antagonists, and equipped, too, with every advantage known to military science, while their own equipment was almost the reverse.

In each of the three cases under consideration, the Confederate lines had been broken and overrun by overwhelming numbers and were now held by the victors exulting in their success. Then the physical condition of the Southern men must not be overlooked. For some days there had scarcely been a lull in the fighting. The small portions of the preceding nights devoted to rest had been passed with their arms and accoutrements about them, and when roused from sleep scant time was given to swallow their rations. Then amid the surroundings of a gloomy forest they moved forward among the wounded and over the dead bodies of their comrades. So if ever environment was such as to allay enthusiasm, surely it was found here.

The following extract from a letter written by Colonel Poague to his father, when these scenes had just transpired, will be of interest:

"Line of battle on Hanover C. H. Road,
"10 miles from Richmond,
"June 1st, 1864.

.   .   .   .   .   .

EXTRACT

"I will take this occasion to relate an incident or two illustrating the feeling our soldiers have for General Lee. On the morning of the 6th of May, when the enemy had gained some advantage over our troops on the plank road in the wilderness and were pressing our men back, Longstreet's troops came up and were hastily formed in line of battle, and as the famous Texas Brigade started forward, passing right through my guns, General Lee rode along with it with head uncovered. This spectacle wrought our troops up to the highest pitch of enthusiasm. But they did not forget that their beloved General was thus greatly exposing himself, and the whole line called out, 'Go back! Go back, General Lee!;' and finally they told him they would not fire a gun unless he went back. Entreated thus by his troops and implored by members of his staff, he was prevailed on to withdraw to a place less exposed. How the old General's heart must have swelled at this display of filial regard and tender solicitude by his veterans under such circumstances! Again at Spottsylvania General Lee was at the position occupied by my battalion, when the Yankee batteries opened most furiously on the place, as if conscious of the whereabouts of their great antagonist. A great big impulsive fellow, private Shirley of Utterbach's battery, becoming uneasy for the safety of the General, politely but earnestly invited him to take a seat in the gunpit. The General in his polite and pleasant way declined. Presently a shell struck very near, covering the General with dirt. Shirley could stand it no longer, but springing forward seized him by the hand and besought him to take a seat in the pit and did almost drag General Lee to a place where he was less exposed. These little incidents will serve to show how General Lee's boys value him and love him. I would not have missed that scene on the plank road for a good deal. But here is an order to move.   .   .   .   .   .

> "Your affectionate son,
>
> "W. T. Poague."

The distinctive features demonstrated on those occasions were: First, General Lee's attitude as he put himself at the head of his men. Then the spirit which animated these men in refusing to allow him to expose his life, and, above all, that it required not even the example of a Lee to encourage them to lay down their lives in the performance of duty.

The South to do honor to itself, and to the memory of these men, should erect a monument which in majesty of proportion and design should have but one competitor, and that one to the mothers and wives in the South, whose self-sacrifice, patience and devotion rendered such deeds of valor only natural.

Much has been said and written concerning the comparative equipment, etc., of the two armies. A striking reference to it I heard in a conversation at General Lee's home in Lexington after the war. Of the students who attended Washington College during his presidency he always requested a visit to himself whenever they returned to the town. With this request they were very ready to comply. While performing this pleasant duty one evening, during a visit to my old home in Lexington, Mrs. Lee, sitting in her invalid-chair, was discoursing to me, feelingly, on the striking contrast between the ragged clothing worn by Confederate soldiers as compared with that worn by the Federals, as she had seen the Federal troops entering Richmond after its evacuation. The General, who was pacing the floor, paused for a moment, his eye lighting up, and, at the conclusion of her remarks, said, as he inclined forward with that superb grace, "But, ah! Mistress Lee, we gave them some awfully hard knocks, with all of our rags!"

After parting with my cadet friends at Hanover Junction, soon after day-dawn, I readily found our battery bivouacking in sight of the station. Some of the men were lying asleep; those who had risen seemed not yet fully awake. All looked ten years older than when I had bidden them good-by a month before—hollow-eyed, unwashed, jaded, and hungry; paper-collars and blue neckties shed and forgotten. The contents of my basket (boxes were now obsolete), consisting of pies, sweetened with sorghum molasses, and other such edibles, were soon devoured, and I reported "returned for duty." In a few hours we were on the road to Richmond, with the prospect of another sojourn in the surrounding swamps.

On the night of June 1 our battery was bivouacked in the edge of a dense piece of woods, the guns being parked in open ground just outside, while the men were lying in the leaves, with the horses tied among them. About midnight one of the horses became tangled in his halter and fell to the ground, struggling and kicking frantically to free himself. A man close by, being startled from sleep, began halloaing, "Whoa, whoa, whoa!" The alarm was taken up by one after another as each roused from slumber, increasing and spreading the noise and confusion; by this time the horses had joined in, pawing and snorting in terror, completing the reign of pandemonium. As darkness prevented successful running, some of the men climbed trees or clung to them for protection, while the sentinel over the guns in the open broke from his beat, supposing Grant's cavalry was upon us. In a space of two minutes all suddenly became still, the climbers stealthily slid from their trees, and others gingerly picked their way back to their lairs, "ashamed as men who flee in battle." For some time, as the cause and absurdity of the incident was realized, there issued now and then from a pile of leaves a chuckle of suppressed laughter.

CHAPTER XXV

AFTER spending the following day and night in "Camp Panic," we moved forward early on the morning of June 3 to the field of the memorable second Cold Harbor. Minie-balls were rapping against the trees as we drove through a copse of small timber to occupy a temporary redoubt in the line of breastworks beyond. While the guns halted briefly before driving in to unlimber, I walked forward to see what was in front. The moment I came into view a Minie-ball sung by my head and passed through the clothes of the cannoneer, Barton Mc-Crum, who was a few steps from me, suggesting to both of us to lie low until called for as videttes. Perched in the tops of the trees beyond the half-mile of open field in our front, the enemy's sharp-shooters, with telescope sights on their rifles, blazed away at every moving object along our line. It was noon before their artillery opened on us, and, in the firing which ensued, a large barn a hundred yards in our front was set on fire by a shell and burned to the ground.

An hour or two later, during this brisk cannonade, I, being No. 3, stood with my thumb on the vent as the gun was being loaded. From a shell which exploded a few yards in front I was struck on the breast by the butt-end, weighing not less than three pounds, and at the same time by a smaller piece on the thigh. After writhing for a time I was accompanied to our surgeon in the rear. The brass button on my jacket, which I still have as a memento, was cut almost in two and the shirt button underneath driven to the breast-bone, besides other smaller gashes. A large contusion was made by the blow on my thigh, and my clothing was very much torn. After my wounds had been dressed I passed the night at the quarters of my friend and fellow-townsman, Capt. Charles Estill, of the Ordnance Department, who already had in charge his brother Jack, wounded in a cavalry engagement the day before.

An hour after dark, as I sat by the light of a camp-fire, enjoying the relief and rest, as well as the agreeable company of old friends, the rattle of musketry two miles away had gradually increased into the proportions of a fierce battle. The feelings of one honorably out of such a conflict, but listening in perfect security, may be better imagined than described. This, like a curfew bell, signaled the close of a day of frightful and probably unparalleled carnage. Within the space of a single hour in the forenoon the Federal army had been three times repulsed with a loss of thirteen thousand men killed and wounded; after which their troops firmly refused to submit themselves to further butchery.

This statement is made on the evidence of Northern historians.

After a night's rest I was sent to Richmond, where I received a transfer to a hospital in Staunton. Sheridan's cavalry having interrupted travel over the Virginia Central Railroad, I went by rail to Lynchburg, via the Southside Road, with Captain Semmes and eight or ten cadets on their return to Lexington with artillery horses pressed into service. Learning, in Lynchburg, that Hunter's army was near Staunton, I continued with the cadets, riding one of their artillery horses, but was too much exhausted to proceed far, and stopped for the night on the way. Here I learned from refugees that Hunter was advancing toward Lexington. As the whole country seemed now to be overrun by the Federals, to avoid them was very difficult.

I resumed my journey toward home, frequently meeting acquaintances who were seeking safety elsewhere. When within four or five miles of the town, while ascending a long hill, I heard the sound of a drum and fife not far ahead. Presently I recognized the tune played to be "Yankee Doodle." I could not believe it to be the vanguard of Hunter's army, but what on earth could it be? However, at the top of the hill I saw a train of refugee wagons preceded by two negroes who were making the music.

I remained at home only a day and a night, at the expiration of which time General McCausland (the first captain of our battery) with his brigade of cavalry was within a mile of town, closely pursued by Hunter's whole army. I spent half of the night assisting my mother and the servants (our slaves) to conceal from the marauders what flour, bacon, etc., the family still had; and before sunrise the next morning set out, mounted on my father's horse, for a safer place. By this time my wounds had become very painful, and my leg had turned a dark-blue color from the thigh to the knee.

A brief account of my experience while refugeeing may be of interest, as it will give an idea of the horror with which our non-combatants regarded the invasion of their homes by our fellow-countrymen of the North, who had now resorted to fire, after learning by bitter experience that the sword alone could not restore us to the blessings of the Union.

My destination was the home of my aunt, Mrs. Allen, forty miles distant, in Bedford County. After passing through the gap between the two peaks of Otter, I reached my aunt's and found there three officers from Louisiana recovering from wounds. After a respite of two days one of the officers, on his return from a neighbor's, brought information that McCausland's command was approaching through the mountain-pass, with Hunter in close pursuit. In a few hours our house of refuge was overrun by McCausland's hungry soldiers. Again I went through the process of helping to hide valuables and packing up what was to be hauled away.

I started at dawn next morning with the officers, leaving my aunt and her three daughters very forlorn and unprotected. When I left she gave me the pistol which her son Robert, colonel of the Twenty-eighth Virginia Regiment, was wearing when he fell in Pickett's charge at Gettysburg. In our care were the loaded wagons, negro men, lowing cows, and bleating sheep.

That afternoon, after exchanging my gray for a fleet-footed cavalry horse ridden by one of the officers, I rode back from our place of hiding, some miles south of Liberty, to reconnoiter; but, after passing through the town, met General McCausland at the head of his brigade falling back toward Lynchburg, and rode back a short distance with him to return to my party of refugees, who meantime had moved farther on. Next day I stopped at a house by the wayside to get dinner, and had just taken my seat at the table when there arose a great commotion outside, with cries of "Yankee cavalry! Yankee cavalry!" Stepping to the door, I saw a stream of terrified school-children crying as they ran by, and refugees flying for the woods. In a moment I was on my fleet-footed dun, not taking time to pick up a biscuit of my untasted dinner nor the pillow worn between my crippled leg and the saddle, and joined in the flight. I had noticed a yearling colt in the yard of the house as I entered, and in five minutes after I started a twelve-year-old boy mounted on the little thing, barebacked, shot by me with the speed of a greyhound. A hundred yards farther on I overtook some refugee wagons from about Lexington, whose owners had left them on the road and betaken themselves to the woods; but there still stood by them a mulatto man of our town—Lindsay Reid by name—who indignantly refused to be routed, and was doing his utmost, with voice and example, to stem the tide, saying, "It is a shame to fear anything; let's stand and give them a fight!"

A moment later a negro boy rode by at a gallop in the direction from which the alarm came. In reply to the inquiry as to where he was going, he called out, "After Marse William." Relying on him as a picket, I remained in view of the road. In ten minutes he appeared, returning at full speed, and called out to me, as he rode up, that he had "run almost into them." They were close behind, and I must "fly or be caught." I was well alongside of him as he finished the warning, and for half a mile our horses ran neck and neck. He said he would take me to his old master's, an out-of-the-way place, several miles distant. Arriving there, a nice country house and very secluded, I concealed my horse in the woods as best I could and went to the house, where I was welcomed and cared for by two young ladies and their aged father, Mr. Hurt, who was blind. I was now much exhausted, and determined to take a rest, with the chances of being captured. The occasion of the alarm was a body of

ROBERT FRAZER

Federal cavalry which had been sent on a raid to meet Hunter's army, advancing on Lynchburg.

After two days in this quiet abode I set out to make my way past the rear of Hunter's army and eventually to reach home. On the way to Liberty I was informed that a train of Hunter's wagons and many negroes, under a cavalry escort, were then passing northward through the town. To satisfy myself (being again mounted on my father's gray) I rode to the top of the hill overlooking the place. Then a strikingly pretty young lady of about sixteen, bareheaded (although it was not then the fashion), and almost out of breath, who had seen me coming into danger, ran to meet me and called, "For God's sake, fly; the town is full of Yankees!" Many years after the war a lady friend of Norfolk, Virginia, who was refugeeing in Liberty at the time, told me that she had witnessed the incident, and said that the girl who had run out to warn me had afterward married a Federal officer. I then went around the town and crossed the road a mile west of it, learning that the wagon-train, etc., had all passed.

From this place on, throughout the territory over which this patriotic army had operated, were the desolated homes of helpless people, stripped of every valuable they possessed, and outraged at the wanton destruction of their property, scarcely knowing how to repair the damage or to take up again their broken fortunes. Night had now fallen, but a bright moon rather added to the risks of continuing my journey. An old negro man, however, kindly agreed to pilot me through fields and woods, avoiding the highways, "as far as Colonel Nichols' " (his master's). When near his destination he went ahead to reconnoiter, and soon returned from the house, accompanied by one of the ladies, who told me that their house and premises had been overrun by Yankees all day, and that some of them were still prowling about, and, in her fright, pointed to each bush as an armed foe.

Camp-fires still burning enabled me to steer clear of the road, but it was midnight when I reached my aunt's, and, going to the negro cabin farthest from her dwelling, I succeeded, after a long time, in getting "Uncle" Mose to venture out of his door. He said he thought the Yankees were all gone, but to wait till he crept up to the house and let "Ole Miss" know I was about. He reported the way clear, and I was soon in the side porch. After the inmates were satisfied as to my identity, the door was opened just enough for me to squeeze through. The family, consisting of females, including the overseer's wife, who had come for protection, quietly collected in the sitting-room, where a tallow candle, placed not to attract attention from outside, shed a dim light over my ghost-like companions clad in their night-dresses. The younger ladies were almost hysterical, and all looked as if they had passed through a fearful storm at sea, as various experiences were recounted. The house had been ransacked from garret to cellar, and what could not be devoured or carried off was scattered about, and such things as sugar, vinegar, flour, salt, etc., conglomerately mixed. The only food that escaped was what the negroes had in their cabins, and this they freely divided with the whites.

The next day I concealed myself and horse in the woods, and was lying half-asleep when I heard footsteps stealthily approaching through the leaves. Presently a half-grown negro, carrying a small basket, stumbled almost on me. He drew back, startled at my question, "What do you want?" and replied, "Nothin'; I jus' gwine take 'Uncle' Mose he dinner. He workin' in de fiel' over yander." My dinner was to be sent by a boy named Phil, so I said, "Is that you, Phil?" "Lordy! Is that you, Marse Eddie? I though you was a Yankee! Yas, dis is me, and here's yer dinner I done brung yer." Phil, who belonged to my aunt, had run off several weeks before, but of his own accord had returned the preceding day, and this was our first meeting.

As Hunter's army was still threatening Lynchburg, to avoid the scouting-parties scouring the country in his rear I set out on Sunday morning to make my way back to Lexington by Peteet's Gap. I was scarcely out of sight—in fact one of my cousins, as I learned afterward, ran to the porch to assure herself that I was gone—when twenty-five or thirty Federal cavalry, accompanied by a large, black dog, and guided by one of my aunt's negroes armed and dressed in Federal uniform, galloped into the yard and searched the house for "rebel soldiers." Passing through the Federal camp-ground, from among the numerous household articles, etc., I picked up a book, on the fly-leaf of which was written, "Captured at Washington College, Lexington, *Rockingham* County, Virginia." That afternoon, as I was slowly toiling up the steep mountain path almost overgrown with ferns, I was stopped by an old, white-bearded mountaineer at a small gate which he held open for me. While asking for the news, after I had dismounted, he noticed the split button on my coat and my torn trousers, and, pausing for a moment, he said, very solemnly, "Well, you ought to be a mighty good young man." I asked why he thought so. "Well," said he, "the hand of God has certainly been around you."

That night I spent at Judge Anderson's, in Arnold's Valley, and the next day reached Lexington —a very different Lexington from the one I had left a fortnight before. The Virginia Military Institute barracks, the professors' houses, and Governor Letcher's private home had been burned, and also all neighboring mills, etc., while the intervening and adjacent grounds were one great desolate common. Preparations had also been made to burn Washington College, when my father, who was a trustee of that institution, called on General Hunter, and, by explaining that it was endowed by and named in honor of General Washington, finally succeeded in preventing its entire destruction, although much valuable apparatus, etc., had already been destroyed.

Comparisons are odious, but the contrast between the conduct of Northern and Southern soldiers during their invasions of each other's territory is very striking and suggestive; especially when taken in connection with the fact that the Federal army, from first to last, numbered twenty-eight hundred thousand men, and the Confederates not more than six hundred and fifty thousand.

General Early, with three divisions, having been despatched from the army near Richmond, had reached Lynchburg in time to prevent its occupancy by Hunter, who promptly retreated, and his army soon became a mass of fugitives, struggling through the mountains of West Virginia on to the Ohio River. The Confederates at Lynchburg, all told, numbered 11,000 men, the Federals 20,000.

An incident which occurred in Rockbridge County, the participants in which were of the "cradle and grave" classes, deserves mention. Maj. Angus McDonald, aged seventy, having four sons in our army, set out from Lexington with his fourteen-year-old son Harry, refugeeing. They were joined, near the Natural Bridge, by Mr. Thomas Wilson, a white-haired old man; and the three determined to give battle to Hunter's army. From a hastily constructed shelter of rails and stones they opened, with shotguns and pistols, on his advance guard, but, of course, were quickly overpowered. Mr. Wilson was left for dead on the ground, and the McDonalds captured. The father was taken to a Northern prison, but Harry made his escape by night in the mountains, and in turn captured a Federal soldier, whom I saw him turn over to the provost on his return to Lexington. General Early pursued Hunter no farther than Botetourt County, and thence passed through Lexington on his disastrous campaign toward Washington.

CHAPTER XXVI

As HAS already been mentioned, the captain under whom the battery was mustered into service was the Rev. Wm. N. Pendleton, rector of the Episcopal Church in Lexington, Virginia, who, after the first battle of Manassas, became chief of artillery of the Army of Northern Virginia. His only son, Alexander S. Pendleton, graduated at Washington College at the age of 18. He entered the army from the University of Virginia at the beginning of the war as lieutenant on General Jackson's staff, and rose through the various grades of promotion to the rank of lieutenant-colonel. After General Jackson's death he continued to fill the position of adjutant to the succeeding commanders of the corps until he fell in battle near Winchester, in 1864. He was one of the bravest and most efficient staff officers in the Army of Northern Virginia.

The captains of the battery under whom I served were three uncommonly brave and capable officers.

The first, William McLaughlin, after making an enviable record with the company, distinguished himself as commander of a battalion of artillery in General Early's company in 1864.

The second, Captain W. T. Poague, whose reputation for efficiency and courage won for him the command of a battalion of artillery in A. P. Hill's corps, was amply equipped with both intelligence and valor to have handled an army division with credit to himself and advantage to the service.

The third, Archibald Graham, who was appointed a sergeant upon the organization of the company, then elected a lieutenant, and for the last two years of the war captain, had the distinction of having been in every engagement in which the battery took part from Hainesville, in 1861, to Appomattox in 1865. His dreamy, brown eyes kindled most at the sound of good music, and where the noise of battle was greatest, and shells flew thickest, there Graham lingered, as if courting danger.

Our First Lieut. W. M. Brown, a brave officer, wounded and captured at Gettysburg, remained in prison from that time until the close of the war.

Lieut. J. B. McCorkle, a noble fellow and recklessly brave, was killed at first Fredericksburg.

As stated in this paper, besides those regularly enrolled in the company were men who did more or less service with it, but whose names do not appear on the roll. For example, Bernard Wolfe, of Martinsburg, served in this capacity for a time previous to and in the first battle of Manassas, and later became major of commissary on General Pendleton's staff.

Chapman Maupin, of Charlottesville, son of Professor Maupin, of the University of Virginia, served during part of the campaign of 1862, was with the battery in several battles, and enlisted afterward in the Signal Corps.

That so many intelligent and educated men from outside of Rockbridge were attracted to this company was primarily due to the fact that the Rev. W. N. Pendleton, its captain until after first Manassas, was a graduate of West Point and was widely known as a clergyman and educator. After his promotion the character of the company itself accomplished the same effect.

Of the names on the roll there were four A. M.'s and a score of students of the University of Virginia. There were at least twenty graduates of Washington College, and as many undergraduates, and many graduates and students of other colleges.

Among the privates in the company was a son and namesake of General R. E. Lee, whose presence in such a capacity was characteristic of his noble father, when it seemed so natural and surely the custom to have provided him with a commission. That the son should have the instincts and attributes of a soldier was not surprising; but, with these inherited gifts, his individuality, in which uniform cheerfulness, consideration for others, and enjoyment of fun were prominent features, won for him the esteem and affection of his comrades. When it fell to his lot, as a cannoneer, to supply temporarily the place of a sick or wounded driver, he handled and cared for his horses as diligently and with as much pride as when firing a gun.

Two sons of Ex-President Tyler, one of whom —Gardiner—afterwards represented his district in Congress.

A son of Commodore Porter, of the United States Navy.

Walter and Joseph Packard, descendants of Charles Lee, who was a brother of Light-Horse Harry Lee.

The beautiful character of Randolph Fairfax, a descendant of Lord Fairfax, who was killed on December 13, 1862, on that fatal hill near Fredericksburg, has been worthily portrayed in a memoir by the Rev. Philip Slaughter. More than ten thousand copies of this memoir were distributed through the army at the expense of General Lee, Gen. J. E. B. Stuart, and other officers and men, and no better idea of the exalted character of young Fairfax can be conveyed, than by extracts copied from this little volume:

" 'REV. P. SLAUGHTER.

" 'DEAR SIR: Please receive enclosed a contribution ($100) to the very laudable work alluded to in church by you to-day. It is very desirable to place the example of Private Randolph Fairfax before every soldier of the army. I am particularly desirous that my command should have the advantage of such a Christian light to guide them on their way. How invincible would an army of such men be!—men who never murmur and who never flinch!

" 'Very truly yours,

" 'J. E. B. STUART.'

"Berkeley Minor says:

" 'I knew Randolph Fairfax at the University quite well, but not so intimately as I did after he joined this company (the Rockbridge Battery). For several months before his death I was his messmate and bedfellow, and was able to note more fully the tone of earnest piety that pervaded his words and actions. He was unselfish, modest, and uniformly kind and considerate to all. If there was one trait in him more striking than others, it was his calm, earnest, trustful demeanor in time of battle, resulting, I believe, from his abiding trust in the providence and love of God. Many fine young men have been removed by death from this company, yet I do not think that any has been more deeply lamented than he.'

"Joseph Packard, another of his comrades, writes:

" 'His cheerful courage, his coolness and steadiness, made him conspicuous in every battlefield. At the battle of Malvern Hill, where he had received a wound which nine men out of ten would have considered an excuse for retiring from the awful scene, he persisted in remaining at his post, and did the work of two until the battery had left the field. But it was in the bearing, more than in the daring, of the soldier's life that his lovely character displayed itself. He never avoided the most trying and irksome duties. If he had selfishness, those who knew him long and well as schoolmates and comrades never discerned it. More than once I have heard his beautiful Christian example spoken of by irreligious comrades. Bitter and inexplicable as may be the Providence which has removed one so full of promise of good to his fellows, I feel that we may thank God that we have been permitted to witness a life so Christ-like terminated by a death so noble.'

"Captain Poague, commanding the Rockbridge Battery, says in a letter to his father:

" 'In simple justice to your son, I desire to express my high appreciation of his noble character as a soldier, a Christian, and gentleman. Modest and courteous in his deportment, charitable and unselfish in his disposition, cheerful and conscientious in his performance of duty, and upright and consistent in his walk and conversation, he was a universal favorite in the company, and greatly beloved by his friends. I don't think I have ever known a young man whose life was so free from the frailties of human nature, and whose character in all aspects formed so faultless a model for the imitation of others. Had his influence been restricted to the silent power and beauty of his example, his life on earth, short as it was, would not have been in vain. The name of Randolph Fairfax will not soon be forgotten by his comrades, and his family may be assured that there are many who, strangers as they are, deeply sympathize with them in their bereavement.'

"The following from General Lee will be a fit climax to the foregoing tributes:

" 'CAMP FREDERICKSBURG, December 28, 1862.

" 'MY DEAR DOCTOR: I have grieved most deeply at the death of your noble son. I have watched his conduct from the commencement of the war, and have pointed with pride to the patriotism, self-denial, and manliness of character he has exhibited. I had hoped that an opportunity would have occurred for the promotion he deserved; not that it would have elevated him, but have shown that his devotion to duty was appreciated by his country. Such an opportunity would undoubtedly have occurred; but he has been translated to a better world for which his purity and his piety have eminently fitted him. You do not require to be told how great his gain. It is the living for whom I sorrow. I beg you will offer to Mrs. Fairfax and your daughters my heartfelt sympathy, for I know the depth of their grief. That God may give you and them strength to bear this great affliction is the earnest prayer of your early friend,

" 'R. E. LEE.

" 'Dr. Orlando Fairfax.' "

A son and two nephews of Hon. A. R. Boteler.
A son of Governor Gilmer, of Virginia.

S. H. Letcher, brother of War-Governor John Letcher.

Mercer Otey, graduate of Virginia Military Institute and son of Bishop Otey, of Tennessee.

Launcelot M. Blackford, A.M., of University of Virginia, who became adjutant of the Twenty-sixth Virginia Infantry, and Superintendent of the Alexandria High School from the close of the war to the present time—forty-one years. He has said to the writer since the war that he cherished the fact of his having been a private in the Rockbridge Artillery with more pride than he felt in any honors he has since achieved.

Robert A. Gibson, of Petersburg, Virginia, now a bishop of Virginia.

Livingston Massie, of Waynesboro, who became captain of another battery and was killed in General Early's battle of Winchester.

Hugh McGuire, of Winchester, brother of Dr. Hunter McGuire, medical director of Jackson's corps, whose gallantry won for him a captaincy in cavalry and lost him his life on the retreat to Appomattox.

Boyd Faulkner, of Martinsburg, son of Hon. Charles J. Faulkner.

Two Bartons from Winchester.

Two Maurys from Jefferson County, Va.

Two Minors from Albemarle and one from Hanover County, Va.

Other members of the company, of whom much

EDWARD H. HYDE
(Color-bearer)

that is interesting could be written, were Edgar and Eugene Alexander, of Moorefield, West Virginia, uncles of the authoress, Miss Mary Johnston. The first named lost an arm at Fredericksburg, the second had his thigh-bone broken at second Manassas.

William H. Bolling, of Petersburg, Virginia, the handsomest of eight handsome brothers and a most polished gentleman.

Holmes Boyd, of Winchester, now a distinguished lawyer of that city.

Daniel Blaine, of Williamsburg, since the war a Presbyterian divine.

Robert Frazer, of Culpeper, an accomplished scholar and prominent educator.

William L. Gilliam, of Powhatan County.

Campbell Heiskell, of Moorfield.

J. K. Hitner, who, though a native of Pennsylvania, fought through the war for the South.

William F. Johnston, of Rockbridge, a sterling man and soldier.

Edward Hyde, of Alexandria, an excellent artist, who devoted most of his time in camp to drawing sketches of army life. He has recently written me that his drawings were lost in a canoe in which he attempted to cross James River on his journey from Appomattox. Otherwise more of them would have appeared in this book.

Otho Kean, of Goochland County, Virginia.

John E. McCauley, of Rockbridge, sergeant of the battery.

William S. McClintic, now a prominent citizen of Missouri.

D. D. Magruder, of Frederick County, Virginia.

Littleton Macon, of Albemarle County, whose utterances became proverbial.

Frank Meade and Frank Nelson, of Albemarle county.

W. C. Gordon, of Lexington, Virginia.

Jefferson Ruffin, of Henrico.

J. M. Shoulder, of Rockbridge.

W. C. Stuart, of Lexington, Virginia.

Stevens M. Taylor, of Albemarle County, Virginia.

Charles M. Trueheart, now a physician in Galveston, Texas.

Thomas M. Wade, of Lexington, Virginia.

W. H. White, of Lexington, Virginia.

Calvin Wilson, of Cumberland County.

John Withrow, of Lexington, Virginia.

William M. Wilson, of Rockbridge, who went by the name of "Billy Zu," abbreviated for zouave; and many other fine fellows, most of whom have long since "passed over the river."

Corporal A. S. Whitt, gunner of the fourth piece, deserves more than casual mention. His clear, blue eye, ruddy complexion, and well-kept beard, and above all his merry laugh, made him attractive. The following incident will recall him most vividly:

Our camp in Orange County, known as "Blue Run Church," occupied a piece of woodland, the

ground sloping to a little ravine along which flowed
a spring-branch, whose pools afforded bowls for
our morning face-washing, and whose source, 100
yards above, delicious drinking water. Approaching the little stream one morning. I came upon Whitt
standing with a foot on either side of it, sleeves
rolled up and shirt collar tucked in, busily engaged.
As he straightened up to greet me, his eyes caught
the sun just risen, and turning toward it, his full
brown beard spangled with the glistening beads of
water, his face lit up with a smile and uplifted
hand, he rolled out in that clear baritone voice:

"Hail! Hail! Smiling morn, smiling morn,
That tips the hills with gold, that tips the hills with gold.
Whose rosy fingers ope the gates of day.
Hail! Hail!"

Grand old Gunner Whitt! who could land a 20-
pound shot within a hair's breadth and not miss.
I doubt not that in a realm where the wild battle-
cry and the wicked scream of shells are unknown,
again and in still richer tones, his salutation is,
"Hail! Hail! All Hail!"

A very interesting personality in our battery was
George Hostetter, a stalwart youth, very erect, with
large, dark eyes. Born and bred in the mountains
of Rockbridge, his surroundings had familiarized
him with the calls of the wild, and to mock the
various birds and animals of the forest was one of
his pastimes. The bugle call for reveille he frequently anticipated by crowing like a rooster, and

ı r

so perfect was the imitation that in the semi-conscious state before waking one would expect to see and hear the ordinary accompaniments of the farm-yard. As my companion on a hunt one morning, his skill (knowledge) in woodcraft served me well. Finding that the small slugs used on partridges were only laughed at by a squirrel, he drew from his pocket and handed me four Minie-balls, which he must have charmed, as with them I brought down three squirrels and a pheasant, but had no such luck on later occasions. After removing his shoes he went stealthily in advance, his shrill whistle being a sure signal that he had "treed."

After serving two years in the battery, Hostetter announced that he was tired of wheeled-guns and would try the infantry and be "sergeant of his own piece," as he expressed it. This he did by exchanging places with a man in the Twenty-seventh Regiment. In the battle of the Wilderness, scorning the protection of breastworks, he advanced to the front, and after ringing out the defiant challenge of a game-cock he would call on the "Yanks to stand up and fight."

Returning to his mountain home at the close of the war his ante-bellum life was resumed until closed after several years by a tragic death. Having taken his gun out one Sunday morning to shoot a marauding fox, he saw a party passing by on their way to church, and with Stonewall Jackson's idea that only the exigencies of war could justify the desecration of the Sabbath, to conceal his gun undertook to drag it. The gun was accidentally discharged, inflicting a mortal wound from which, after a week's suffering, he died.

In this company were all classes of society and all grades of intelligence, from the most cultured scholars to the lowest degree of illiteracy. We had men who had formerly been gentlemen of leisure, lawyers, physicians, students of divinity, teachers, merchants, farmers and mechanics, ranging in age from boys of seventeen to matured men in the forties and from all parts of the South and several from Northern States, as well as Irish and Germans. At one camp-fire could be heard discussions on literature, philosophy, science, etc., and at another horse-talk. The tone of the company was decidedly moral, and there was comparatively little profanity. In addition to the services conducted by the chaplain of the battalion, Rev. Henry White, prayer-meetings were regularly held by the theological students. Then we had men that swore like troopers. "Irish Emmett," whose face was dotted with grains of powder imbedded under the skin, could growl out oaths through half-clenched teeth that chilled one's blood.

One man, Michael, a conscript from another county, a full-grown man, weighing perhaps one hundred and seventy-five pounds, was a chronic cry-baby; unfit for other service, he was assigned assistant at the forge, and would lie with face to the ground and moan out, "I want to go home, I want to go home," and sob by the hour.

Another, a primitive man from the German forests, whose language was scarcely intelligible, lived entirely to himself and constructed his shelter of brush and leaves—as would a bear preparing to hibernate. In his ignorance of the use of an axe I saw him, in felling a tree, "throw" it so that it fell on and killed a horse tied nearby. On seeing what he had done, his lamentation over the dying animal was pathetic.

The death of this horse was peculiar. I have seen horses wounded and mutilated in every degree of severity—some partially disemboweled, but still on their feet, turning round and round in one spot, till they lay down to die; others with great furrows plowed along their backs or sides, others still, with a leg shot away, tossing the head up and down as they labored to follow on, but all too brave to utter other than a half-suppressed groan. But this old gray went down with a piercing cry, which besides giving expression to intense pain seemed a rebuke as well to the stupidity of the man, who had brought him, after having lived through so many fierce battles, to such an ignoble end.

As a school for the study of human nature, that afforded in the various conditions of army life is unsurpassed—a life in which danger, fatigue, hunger, etc., leave no room for dissimulation, and expose the good and bad in each individual to the knowledge of his associates.

It sometimes fell to my lot to be on guard-duty with Tom Martin, an Irishman who was over forty-five and exempt from military service, but was soldiering for the love of it. Sometimes he was very taciturn and entirely absorbed with his short-stemmed pipe; at other times full of humor and entertaining. He gave me an account, one night while on post, of what he called his "great flank movement"—in other words, a visit to his home in Rockbridge without leave. After Doran, another Irishman, had been disabled at Malvern Hill and discharged from service, he became a sort of huckster for the battery and would make trips to and from Rockbridge with a wagon-load of boxes from our homes and also a supply of apple-brandy. While camped at Bunker Hill in the fall of 1862, shortly after Doran arrived with his load, Captain Poague, observing more than an ordinary degree of hilarity among some of the men, had the wagon searched, the brandy brought forth, confiscated, and emptied on the ground. Martin, greatly outraged at the ill-treatment of a fellow-son of Erin, and still more so at the loss of so much good liquor, forthwith resolved to take his revenge on the Captain by taking "French leave."

To escape the vigilance of provost-guards and deserter-hunters, he made his way to the foothills of the North Mountain, and in the course of his journey stumbled on a still-house in one of its secluded glens. To the proprietor, who was making a run of apple-brandy, and who proved to be "a man after me own heart," Martin imparted his grievances. "I tould him," he said, "I hadn't a cint, but he poured me a tin chuck-full. With thanks in me eyes I turned off the whole of it, then kindled me pipe and stood close by the still. Ah! me lad, how the liquor wint through me! In thray minits I didn't care a domn for all the captins in old Stonewall's army!"

With various adventures he made his way home, returned to the company of his own accord, was wounded at Gettysburg, captured, and spent the remainder of war-time in prison.

Rader, who drove the lead-horses at my gun almost throughout the war, is mentioned elsewhere, but his record, as well as his pranks and drollery, coupled with his taciturnity, were interesting. While sitting on his saddle-horse in one battle he was knocked full length to the ground by a bursting shell. When those nearby ran to pick him up they asked if he was much hurt. "No," he said, "I am just skeered to death." At Sharpsburg, while lying down, holding his gray mares, a shell tore a trench close alongside of him and hoisted him horizontally into the air. On recovering his feet he staggered off, completely dazed by the concussion. In the first battle of Fredericksburg he was struck and disabled for a time. At Gettysburg, as the same animals, frightened by a bursting shell, wheeled to run, he seized the bridle of the leader just as it was struck by a shell, which burst at the moment, instantly killing the two grays and the two horses next to them, and stunning Rader as before. But, with all of his close calls, his skin was never broken. Instead of currying his horses during the time allotted for that work he seemed to occupy himself teaching them "tricks," but his was the best-groomed team in the battery.

While on guard one cold night, as the wagon drivers were sleeping quietly on a bed of loose straw near a blazing fire, I saw Rader creep up stealthily and apply a torch at several places, wait until it was well ignited, and then run and yell "Fire!" then repeat the sport an hour later. Vanpelt carried an enormous knapsack captured from Banks and branded "10th Maine." While halting on the march it was Rader's amusement, especially when some outsider was passing by, to set his whip-stock as a prop under it, go through the motions of grinding, and rattle off the music of a hand-organ with his mouth until chased away by his victim. He mysteriously vanished from Rockbridge after the war, and has never since been located.

Few men in this battery made a finer record than did Wm. H. McCampbell, a native of Lexington, and since the war a resident of Roanoke County, Va. He took part in every engagement from Hainesville in '61 to Appomattox in '65, except Malvern Hill, when he was in hospital. He was twice wounded, captured at Gettysburg and escaped, and is probably entitled to the distinction of having "pulled the lanyard" oftener, that is fired more shots, than any other cannoneer in the whole army.

One of the most striking characters in the company was "General" Jake, as we called him, whose passion for war kept him always in the army, while his aversion to battle kept him always in the rear. After serving a year with us, being over military age, he got a discharge, but soon joined the Rockbridge cavalry as a substitute, where six legs, instead of two, afforded three-fold opportunities. An interview between the "General" and one of our company, as he viewed the former and was struck with his appearance, was as follows:

"Well, 'General,' you are the most perfect-looking specimen of a soldier I ever beheld. That piercing eye, the grizzly mustache, the firm jaw, the pose of the head, that voice—in fact, the whole make-up fills to the full the measure of a man of war."

The "General," with a graceful bow and a deep roll in his voice, replied, "Sire, in enumerating the items which go to constitute a great general I notice the omission of one requisite, the absence of which in my outfit lost to the cause a genius in council and a mighty leader in battle."

"What was that, 'General'!"

"Sire, it goes by the name of Cour-ridge."

Estimates of things are governed by comparison, and no better idea of the Southern army could be had than that given by a knowledge of its numbers, equipment, etc., as compared with those of its adversary throughout the four years of the war. This can be illustrated by a sketch of the Rockbridge Artillery in that respect, beginning with its entrance into service, as a type of the whole army.

The guns with which this company set out from Lexington were two smooth-bore six-pound brass pieces used by Stonewall Jackson for drilling the cadets at the Virginia Military Institute, which were coupled together and drawn by one pair of horses to Staunton. I must pause here and relate an incident which occurred at that period, in which these guns played a part. Among the cadets was one—Hountsell—who was considered as great an enigma as Jackson himself. In some of the various evolutions of the drill it was necessary for the cadets to trot. This gait Hountsell failed to adopt, and was reported to the superintendent with the specification "for failing to trot." Hountsell handed in his written excuse as follows, "I am reported by Major Jackson for failing, at artillery drill, to trot. My excuse is, I am a natural pacer." It would be interesting to know the workings of Stonewall's mind when perusing this reply.

After reaching Harper's Ferry two more six-pound brass pieces were received for this battery from Richmond. As there were no caissons for these four guns, farm-wagons were used, into which boxes of ammunition, together with chests containing rations for the men, were loaded. In addition to friction-primers of modern invention at that time for firing cannon, the old-time "slow matches" and "port-fires" were in stock. So that, in preparing for battle with General Patterson's army at Haines-ville on July 2, 1861, the ammunition-boxes, provision-chests, etc., being loaded indiscriminately into the same wagon, were all taken out and placed on the ground. The "port-fire," adjusted in a brass tube on the end of a wooden stick, was lighted, and the stick stuck in the ground by the gun, to give a light in case the friction-primer failed. This provision was due to the fact that Captain Pendleton was familiar with the "port-fire," in vogue when he attended West Point. On finding that the friction-primer was reliable, the "port-fires" were left sticking in the ground when the guns withdrew, and were captured and taken as curiosities by the Federals.

After returning to Winchester, ammunition-chests were ordered to be made by a carpenter of the town. Gen. Joe Johnston, then in command of the forces, went in person with Lieutenant Poague, and, as the latter expressed it, reprimanded this carpenter most unmercifully for his tardiness in the work. The chests were then quickly completed and placed on wagon-gears, which outfits served as caissons, and thus equipped the battery marched to and fought at first Manassas. From captures there made, these crude contrivances were replaced with regular caissons, and for two of the six-pound brass pieces two rifled ten-pound Parrotts were substituted and two heavier six-pound brass pieces added, making a six-gun battery. Also the farm-wagon harness was exchanged for regular artillery harness.

The revolution in the character of Confederate field ordnance thenceforward continued, and every new and improved weapon we had to confront in one battle we had to wield against our foes, its inventors, in the next.

For a short time previous to and in the battle of Kernstown the battery had eight guns, two of which, made at the Tredegar Works in Richmond, were of very inferior quality and were soon discarded. The long and trying campaign of 1862 gradually reduced the number of guns to four, two of which were twenty-pound Parrotts captured at Harper's Ferry, one a twelve-pound Napoleon captured at Richmond, and one a six-pound brass piece. The two last were replaced by two more twenty-pound Parrotts captured from Milroy at Winchester in June, 1863. Each of these guns required a team of eight horses and as many to a caisson. They were recaptured at Deep Bottom below Richmond in July, 1864.

The battery's connection with the Stonewall Brigade was severed October 1, at the close of the memorable campaign of 1862, and under the new régime became a part of the First Regiment Virginia Artillery, commanded by Col. J. Thompson Brown, afterward by Col. R. A. Hardaway. This regiment was made up of the second and third companies of

Richmond Howitzers, the Powhatan battery commanded by Captain Dance, the Roanoke battery
commanded by Captain Griffin, and Rockbridge battery commanded by Captain Graham, with four
guns to each of the five batteries.

Our new companions proved to be a fine lot of
men, and with them many strong and lasting friend-
ships were formed.

An idea of the spirit with which the Southern
people entered into the war can best be conveyed by
some account of the wild enthusiasm created by the
troops and the unbounded hospitality lavished upon
them as they proceeded to their destinations along
the border.

The Rockbridge Artillery traveled by rail from
Staunton to Strasburg. On their march of eighteen
miles from there to Winchester they were preceded
by the "Grayson Dare-devils" of Virginia, one hundred strong, armed with Mississippi rifles and wearing red-flannel shirts. A mile or two in advance of
this company was the Fourth Alabama Regiment,
numbering eight hundred men. The regiment, on
its arrival at Newtown, a small village six miles
from Winchester, was provided by the citizens with
a sumptuous dinner. Then the "Dare-devils" were
likewise entertained; but still the supplies and hospitality of the people were not exhausted, as the
battery, on its arrival, was served with a bountiful
meal.

When the battery reached Winchester their two

small guns were stored for the night in a warehouse, and the men lodged and entertained in private houses. On the following day the company went by rail to Harper's Ferry, arriving there after dark. The place was then under command of Col. T. J. Jackson, who was soon after superseded by Gen. Joseph E. Johnston. The trains over the B. & O. Railroad were still running. Evidences of the John Brown raid were plainly visible, and the engine-house in which he and his men barricaded themselves and were captured by the marines, commanded by Col. R. E. Lee, of the United States Army, stood as at the close of that affair.

One or both sections of the battery were often engaged in picket service along the Potomac between Sheperdstown and Williamsport, in connection with the Second Virginia Regiment, which was composed of men from the adjoining counties. Their camps and bivouacs were constantly visited by the neighboring people, especially ladies, who came by the score in carriages and otherwise, provided with abundant refreshments for the inner man. As described by those who participated in it all, the days passed as a series of military picnics, in which there was no suspicion or suggestion of the serious times that were to follow. During the progress of the war, while these outward demonstrations, of necessity, diminished, the devotion on the part of the grand women of that war-swept region only increased.

I have not undertaken to describe scenes or relate incidents which transpired in the battery before I became a member of it. But there is one scene which was often referred to by those who witnessed it which is worthy of mention. It occurred in the fall of 1861, near Centerville, when a portion of the army, under Gen. Joe Johnston, was returning from the front, where an attack had been threatened, and was passing along the highway. A full moon was shining in its splendor, lighting up the rows of stacked arms, parks of artillery, and the white tents which dotted the plain on either side. As column after column, with bands playing and bayonets glistening, passed, as it were, in review, there came, in its turn, the First Maryland Regiment headed by its drum corps of thirty drums rolling in martial time. Next came the First Virginia Regiment with its superb band playing the "Mocking-Bird," the shrill strains of the cornet, high above the volume of the music, pouring forth in exquisite clearness the notes of the bird. Scarcely had this melody passed out of hearing when there came marching by, in gallant style, the four batteries of the Washington Artillery, of New Orleans, with officers on horseback and cannoneers mounted on the guns and caissons, all with sabers waving in cadence to the sound of their voices, singing, in its native French, "The Marseillaise," that grandest of all national airs.

The younger generation cannot comprehend, and express surprise that the old soldiers never forget and are so wrought up by the recollections of their war experiences; but to have participated in a scene such as this will readily explain why a soul should thrill at its recurring mention.

In 1883, nearly twenty years after the war, I was called to Cumberland, Maryland, on business. By reason of a reunion of the Army of the Cumberland being held there at the time, the hotels were crowded, making it necessary for me to find accommodations in a boarding-house. Sitting around the front door of the house, as I entered, were half a dozen Federal soldiers discussing war-times. The window of the room to which I was assigned opened immediately over where the men sat, and as I lay in bed I heard them recount their experiences in battle after battle in which I had taken part. It stirred me greatly. Next morning they had gone out when I went down to breakfast, but I told the lady of the house of my interest in their talk of the previous night. At noon the same party was sitting in the hall, having finished their dinners, as I passed through to mine. They greeted me cordially and said, "We heard of what you said about overhearing us last night; take a seat and let's discuss old times." My answer was, "I have met you gentlemen already on too many battle-fields with an empty stomach, so wait till I get my dinner." With a hearty laugh this was approved of, and I joined them soon after. Most of them were from Ohio and West Virginia. They said, though, as I was but one against six, to say what I pleased;

and for an hour or more we discussed, good-humoredly, many scenes of mutual interest.

The following lines are recalled from Merrick's songs:

"Och hone, by the man in the moon!
  You taze me all ways that a woman can plaze;
  For you dance twice as high with that thief, Pat
      McGhee,
  As you do when you're dancing a jig, Love, with
      me;
  Though the piper I'd bate, for fear the old chate
  Wouldn't play you your favorite chune.

"Och hone, don't provoke me to do it,
  For there are girls by the score
  That would have me and more.
  Sure there's Katy Nale, that would jump if I'd say,
  'Katy Nale, name the day.'
  And though you are fresh and fair as the flowers
      in May,
  And she's short and dark as a cowld winter's day,
  If you don't repent before Easter, when Lent
  Is over, I'll marry for spite."

SAINT PATRICK

"A fig for St. Denis of France!
  He's a trumpery fellow to brag on.
A fig for St. George and his lance!
  Who splitted a heathenish dragon.

The saints of the Welshman and Scot
　Are a pair of pitiful pipers,
Both of whom may just travel to pot,
　Compared with the patron of swipers—
St. Patrick of Ireland, my boy!

"Och! he came to the Emerald Isle
　On a lump of a paving-stone mounted;
The steamboat he beat by a mile,
　Which mighty good sailing was counted.
Said he, 'The salt-water, I think,
　Makes me most bloodily thirsty,
So fetch me a flagon of drink
　To wash down the mullygrubs, burst ye!
A drink that is fit for a saint.'

"The pewter he lifted *in sport,*
　And, believe me, I tell you no fable,
A gallon he drank from the quart
　And planted it down on the table.
'A miracle!' every one cried,
　And they all took a pull at the stingo.
They were capital hands at the trade,
　And they drank till they fell; yet, by jingo!
The pot still frothed over the brim.

" 'Next day,' quoth his host, 'is a fast
　And there is naught in my larder but mutton.
On Friday who would serve such repast,
　Except an unchristianlike glutton?'

18

Says Pat, 'Cease your nonsense, I beg;
    What you tell me is nothing but gammon.
Take my compliments down to the leg
    And bid it walk hither, a salmon.'
The leg most politely complied.

"Oh! I suppose you have heard, long ago,
    How the snakes, in a manner quite antic,
He marched from the County Mayo
    And trundled them into the Atlantic.
So not to use water for drink,
    The people of Ireland determined.
And for a mighty good reason, I think,
    Since St. Patrick has filled it with vermin
And vipers and other such stuff.

.   .   .   .

"The people, with wonderment struck
    At a pastor so pious and civil,
Cried, 'We are for you, my old buck!
    And we'll pitch our blind gods to the devil
Who dwells in hot water below.'

"Och! he was an iligant blade
    As you'd meet from Fairhead to Killkrumper,
And, though under the sod he is laid,
    Here goes his health in a bumper!
I wish he was here, that my glass
    He might, by art-magic, replenish—
But as he is not, why, alas!
    My ditty must come to a finish,
Because all the liquor is out."

JOHN M. BROWN

THE SECOND ROCKBRIDGE ARTILLERY

The Second Rockbridge Artillery Company, organized July 10, 1861, like the first Rockbridge Artillery, was commanded by a clergyman, the Rev. John Miller, of Princeton, New Jersey, as captain. In honor of his wife's sister, Miss Lily McDowell, daughter of Governor McDowell, of Virginia, who furnished in large part the outfit of this company, it was named "McDowell Guards." She also paid a bounty to a youth under military age to serve as her personal representative in this company. Miss McDowell afterward became the wife of Major Bernard Wolfe, whose service with the Rockbridge Battery has been mentioned.

Owing to lack of artillery equipment, the McDowell Guards served as infantry until January, 1862, in the Fifty-second Virginia Regiment, in West Virginia. I heard Captain Miller relate this anecdote, which occurred in the battle of Alleghany Mountain, December 12, 1861: A boy in his company was having a regular duel with a Federal infantryman, whose shots several times passed close to the boy's head. Finally, when a bullet knocked his hat off, he defiantly called out to his adversary, "Hey! You didn't git me that time, nuther. You didn't git me nary a time!"

In the early part of 1862 the McDowell Guards secured artillery and did excellent service in McIntosh's battalion of A. P. Hill's corps until the close of the war.

CHAPTER XXVII

OAKLAND—RETURN TO CAMP—OFF DUTY AGAIN—
THE RACE FROM NEW MARKET TO FORT GIL-
MORE—ATTACK ON FORT HARRISON—WINTER-
QUARTERS ON THE LINES—VISITS TO RICHMOND

THE desolation and dejection of the people of
Lexington hastened my departure, but before returning to the army I spent two weeks most delightfully
at "Oakland," the hospitable home of Mrs. Cocke,
in Cumberland County, Virginia. This was the last
opportunity I had of enjoying the "old plantation
life," the like of which can never again be experienced. It was an ideal life, the comforts and advantages of which only those who followed it could
appreciate. Two of Mrs. Cocke's sons, who had
passed many years at school and college in Lexington, were at home—one on sick-leave; the other,
still a youth, equipping himself for the cavalry service, which he soon entered. William, the eldest
son, had been killed at Gettysburg and his body never
recovered.

Every day at twelve o'clock sharp, delicious water-
melons were brought from the icehouse to the shade
of the stately oaks which adorned the spacious lawn;
then, two hours later, after a sumptuous dinner, a
small darky brought from the kitchen a shovel of

274

coals (matches were not a Southern product) to light our pipes. So the time passed. It was to this hospitable home that General Lee retired with his family immediately after Appomattox, and was living on this estate when he accepted the presidency of Washington College.

My wounds being now sufficiently, or rather temporarily, healed, I embarked about bedtime at Cartersville on the canal packet boat. On my way to a berth in the cabin I noticed, by the dim light, a striking-looking man clad in white lying in his berth. On the deck of the boat were a score or more of negroes, male and female, singing so boisterously that the other passengers could not sleep. Such conduct at this time was felt to be significant, and the more so as the officers of the boat refrained from interfering. Without intimation there was a leap from my neighboring bunk, a hurried scramble up the stairway, followed by a volley of—secular language, with a demand for instantaneous choice between "dead silence and dead niggers." Thenceforward stillness prevailed, broken at intervals when the plaintive windings of the packet horn, rising and falling with the motion of the tandem team, heralded our approach to a lock. Who that ever boarded that ancient craft, or dwelt within its sound, will cease to recall the associations awakened by the voice of the old packet horn?

Next morning I recognized my fellow-countryman, Bob Greenlee, of the First Virginia Cavalry, as the man whose eloquence had terrorized the negroes. Greenlee has been aptly styled "a rare bird," and the accounts he gave of experiences during his sick-leave, from which he was now returning, were as good as "David Harum."

I found the battery stationed at New Market, on the north side of the James, near Dutch Gap. During my absence it had suffered the only serious loss of the kind it had experienced during the war—the capture of all four of its twenty-pound Parrott guns at Deep Bottom. The horses, as usual, had been taken to the rear for safety. The infantry support had been outflanked, leaving our guns almost surrounded, so that the cannoneers escaped with difficulty—only one of them, Andrew Darnall, being captured.

The ranks of the company had been considerably depleted by chills and fever, so prevalent in that swampy region, and one death had occurred—that of John Gibbs, a most excellent soldier. Less than a week's sojourn was sufficient to poison my blood and reopen an old wound received two years before. I was sent to Richmond, but twenty-four hours' experience in a hospital among the sick, the wounded, and the dying induced me to get a discharge and work my way, by hook and crook, back to Oakland, where I underwent a severe visitation of chills and fever. This, however, was soon broken up by quinine, and I again rejoined the battery.

The summer now drawing to a close had been a most trying one, and the future offered no sign of relief. The situation was one of simply waiting to be overwhelmed. That the fighting spirit was unimpaired was demonstrated in every encounter, notably the one on July 30, at The Crater, near Petersburg.

During the night of September 28 there was heard the continued rumbling of wheels and the tramp of large forces of the enemy crossing on the pontoon bridges from the south to north side of the James. At dawn next morning we hurriedly broke camp, as did Gary's brigade of cavalry camped close by, and scarcely had time to reach high ground and unlimber before we were attacked. The big gaps in our lines, entirely undefended, were soon penetrated, and the contest quickly became one of speed to reach the shorter line of fortifications some five miles nearer to and in sight of Richmond. The break through our lines was on our right, which placed the Federals almost in our rear, so that a detour of several miles on our part was necessary. On the principle that the chased dog is generally the fleetest, we succeeded in reaching the breastworks, a short distance to the left of Fort Gilmore, with all four guns, now ten-pound Parrotts, followed by the straggling cannoneers much exhausted. I vividly recall George Ginger, who was No. 1 at one of the guns, as he came trotting in with the gun-rammer on his shoulder, which he had carried five miles through brush and brake for want of time to replace it on the gun-carriage.

Much has been written about the defense of Fort Gilmore, and much controversy as to who deserved the credit. The fact that a superb fight was made was fully apparent when we entered the fort an hour later, while the negroes who made the attack were still firing from behind stumps and depressions in the cornfield in front, to which our artillery replied with little effect. The Fort was occupied by about sixty men who, I understood, were Mississippians. The ditch in front was eight or ten feet deep and as many in width. Into it, urged on by white officers, the negroes leaped, and to scale the embankment on the Fort side climbed on each other's shoulders, and were instantly shot down as their heads appeared above it. The ground beyond was strewn with dead and wounded. A full regiment had preceded us into the Fort, but the charge on it had been repulsed by the small force before its arrival.

Next morning we counted twenty-three dead negroes in the ditch, the wounded and prisoners having previously been removed. There was great lamentation among them when "Corporal Dick" fell. He was a conspicuous leader, jet black, and bald as a badger. A mile to the right of Fort Gilmore and one-fourth of a mile in advance of our line of breastworks was Fort Harrison, which was feebly garrisoned by reserves. This force had been overpowered and the Fort taken by the Federals. Two days later, and after it had been completely manned with infantry and artillery, an unsuccessful attempt was made to recapture it, of which we had a full view. The attack was made by Colquitt's and Anderson's brigades, while General Lee stood on the parapet of Fort Gilmore with field-glass in hand, waving his hat and cheering lustily. Of course our loss in killed, wounded, and captured was very heavy. This ended the fighting, except sharpshooting, on the north side of the James.

During our stay in Fort Gilmore a company of Reserves from Richmond took the place of the regular infantry. They were venerable-looking old gentlemen—lawyers, business men, etc., dressed in citizens' clothes. In order to accustom them to the service, we supposed, they were frequently roused during the night to prepare for battle. After several repetitions of this they concluded, about two o'clock one night, that it was useless to retire again and go through the same performance, so a party of them kindled a fire and good-humoredly sat around in conversation on various subjects, one of which was infant baptism. My bedfellow, Tom Williamson, a bachelor under twenty years of age, being deeply interested in this question, of paramount importance at this time, forthwith left his bunk, and from that time until daylight theology was in the air.

Our battery changed from the Fort to a position one-fourth of a mile to the left of it, the two sections being placed a hundred yards apart, where we remained until March.

It seems remarkable even now, after a lapse of over forty years, that under such conditions and without the slightest reasonable hope of ultimate success we could have passed six months, including a severe winter, not only moderately comfortable, but ofttimes with real pleasure. Huts and hovels of as varied architecture as the scarcity of material at our disposal could be shaped into, rose above or descended below the ground. The best shelters were built of pine logs six or eight inches in diameter, split in half, with the bark-side out. From a swamp a quarter of a mile in the rear, in which the trees had been previously felled for military operations, we carried our fuel. Several hundred negroes had been impressed, in neighboring counties within Confederate lines, to work on the adjacent fortifications, which, by their industry, soon became very strong. In our immediate front, manning the Federal works, were negro troops whose voices could be distinctly heard in darky songs and speech, and their camp-fires were in full view.

It was at this time that General Early was distinguishing himself in the Shenandoah Valley with repeated defeats in battle, the first news of which reached us in a peculiar way; that is, when the news reached Grant's lines a shotted salute in celebration was fired at us, thus "killing two birds with one stone." These volleys of shot and shell produced consternation among the negroes working on our fortifications. Panic-stricken, they would break for the rear, casting aside picks, shovels, or anything that retarded speed; and to get them and their scattered tools gathered up after such a stampede required several days. I was requested, by a negro who had just experienced one of these escapades, to write a letter for him to his home people. He dictated as follows:

"My dear Wife: I take this opportunity of taking you down a few words and telling you of the terrible bumming we was under yesterday. The shells fell fast as hail and lightened as from a cloud —and we had a smart run. Give my love to Mammy and tell her how we is sufferin' for somethin' to eat."

Then followed some other pieces of news; then love to various kinsmen, with a message to each of how they were "sufferin' for somethin' to eat."

The space between the two sections of our battery was occupied by infantry. I particularly remember the Nineteenth Georgia Regiment, a game body of men, whose excellent band furnished us fine music. It was ordered, during the winter, to North Carolina and lost—killed in battle soon after—its colonel and adjutant, Neil and Turner. A mile in rear of our lines stood a church, a substantial frame building, which, for want of better use, was converted into a theater. As in the recent drafting every department of life had been invaded, a very respectable element of a histrionic turn was to be found in the ranks. The stage scenery, as one would imagine, was not gaudy and, of course, did not afford equipment for high art in the strict sense; but the doleful conditions of home life now in vogue in the South and the desperate straits for food and existence in camp afforded a fund of amusement to those of us who were inclined to pluck sport from hopeless conditions.

One of the performers—named Nash—was a first-rate comedian. As an interlude he gave a representation of an attempt made by the people to furnish the army a Christmas dinner. To give an idea of what a failure such an undertaking would naturally be, when the people themselves were almost destitute, one thin turkey constituted the share for a regiment close by us, while our battery did not get so much as a doughnut. Nash, in taking the thing off, appeared on the stage with a companion to propound leading questions, and, after answering one query after another, to explain the meaning of his droll conduct, drew his hand from the side pocket of his blouse and, with his head thrown back and mouth wide open, poured a few dry cracker crumbs down his throat. When asked by the ringman what that act signified, he drawled out, in lugubrious tones, "Soldier eating Christmas dinner!" The righteous indignation produced among the few citizens by such sacrilegious use of a church soon brought our entertainments to a close.

Our time was frequently enlivened by visits to

Richmond. By getting a twenty-four-hour leave we could manage to spend almost forty-eight hours in the city. On a pass—dated, for instance, January 13—we could leave camp immediately after reveille and return in time for reveille on the fifteenth.

That this would be the last winter that Richmond would be the capital of the Confederacy, or that the Confederacy itself would be in existence, was a feeling experienced by all, but was too painful a subject for general discussion. The gaiety of the place under such conditions, viewed at this remote day, seems astonishing. There the Confederate Congress and the Virginia Legislature held their sessions; and there were the numerous employees of State and Nation, and refugees from various parts of the South, and, besides, it was the great manufacturing center of that section, employing mechanics and artisans of every calling. For four years this mixed multitude had listened to the thunder of cannon almost at their doors, and had seen old men and boys called out by day and by night to meet some extraordinary emergency, while it was no uncommon occurrence for hundreds of sick, wounded, and dead men to be borne through the streets to the overflowing hospitals and cemeteries. One surprising feature of it was to see how readily all adapted themselves to such a life.

My first social visit, in company with my messmate, James Gilmer, of Charlottesville, Virginia, was to call on some lady friends, formerly of Winchester. We found these ladies starting to an eggnog at the house of some friends—the Misses Munford—with instructions to invite their escorts. This position we gladly accepted, and were soon ushered into the presence of some of the celebrated beauties of Richmond, and were entertained as graciously as if we had been officers of high rank. The climax of this visit was as we were returning to camp the next afternoon. We overtook Tazewell McCorkle, of Lynchburg, the only member of our company who could afford the luxury of being married and having his wife nearby. He had just received a box from home, and invited us to go with him to his wife's boarding-house and partake of its contents. While enjoying and expressing our appreciation of the good things, McCorkle told us of the impression the sight of old-time luxuries had made on their host, Mr. Turner, a devout old Baptist, who, with uplifted hands, exclaimed, as it first met his gaze, "Pound-cake, as I pray to be saved!"

Since the burning of the Virginia Military Institute barracks, by Hunter at Lexington, the school had been transferred to Richmond and occupied the almshouse. This, on my visits to the city, I made my headquarters, and, preparatory to calling on my lady acquaintances, was kindly supplied with outfits in apparel by my friends among the professors. Having developed, since entering the service, from a mere youth in size to a man of two hundred

RANDOLPH FAIRFAX

pounds, to fit me out in becoming style was no simple matter. I recall one occasion when I started out on my visiting-round, wearing Frank Preston's coat, Henry Wise's trousers, and Col. John Ross's waistcoat, and was assured by my benefactors that I looked like a brigadier-general. Sometimes as many as four or six of our company, having leave of absence at the same time, would rendezvous to return together in the small hours of the night, through Rocketts, where "hold-ups" were not uncommon, and recount our various experiences as we proceeded campward.

Indications of the hopelessness of the Confederacy had, by midwinter, become very much in evidence, with but little effort at concealment. Conferences on the subject among the members of companies and regiments were of almost daily occurrence, in which there was much discussion as to what course should be pursued when and after the worst came. Many resolutions were passed in these meetings, avowing the utmost loyalty to the cause, and the determination to fight to the death. In one regiment not far from our battery a resolution was offered which did not meet the approbation of all concerned, and was finally passed in a form qualified thus, "Resolved, that in case our army is overwhelmed and broken up, we will bushwack them; —— that is, some of us will."

Notwithstanding all this apprehension, scant rations and general discomfort, the pluck and spirit

of the great majority of our men continued un-
abated. To give an idea of the insufficiency of the
rations we received at this time, the following incident which I witnessed will suffice: Immediately
after finishing his breakfast, one of our company
invested five dollars in five loaves of bread. After
devouring three of them, his appetite was sufficiently appeased to enable him to negotiate the exchange of one of the two remaining for enough
molasses to sweeten the other, which he ate at once.
These loaves, which were huckstered along the
lines by venders from Richmond, it must be understood, were not full-size, but a compromise between
a loaf and a roll.

The frequent occasions of foraging and stress
laid on eating, in these pages, has doubtless been
noticed and very naturally and inquiringly by those
whose lives have had no such experience. A simple
extract quoted from a Northern source—"Recollections of a Private Soldier in the Army of the
Potomac," by Frank Wilkeson—will suffice. It
reads: "I was hungry—it seems now, as I recall
those dark and bloody days, I was always hungry."

Desertions were of almost nightly occurrence,
and occasionally a half-dozen or more of the infantry on the picket line would go over in a body
to the enemy and give themselves up. The Federals, who had material and facilities for pyrotech-
nic displays, one night exhibited in glaring letters
of fire:

"While the lamp holds out to burn,
The vilest rebel may return."

Toward the latter part of March our battery moved half a mile back of the line of breastworks. Two or more incidents recall, very distinctly to my memory, the camp which we there occupied. The colored boy Joe, who had cooked for my mess when rations were more abundant, was on hand again to pay his respects and furnish music for our dances. If we had been tramping on a hard floor never a sound of his weak violin could have been heard; but on the soft, pine tags we could go through the mazes of a cotillion, or the lancers, with apparently as much life as if our couples had been composed of the two sexes. The greatest difficulty incurred, in having a game of ball, was the procurement of a ball that would survive even one inning. One fair blow from the bat would sometimes scatter it into so many fragments that the batter would claim that there were not enough remains caught by any one fielder to put him out.

CHAPTER XXVIII

EVACUATION OF RICHMOND—PASSING THROUGH
RICHMOND BY NIGHT—THE RETREAT—BATTLE
OF SAILOR'S CREEK—BATTLE OF CUMBERLAND
CHURCH

WHILE here, in the midst of our gaiety, came the
news of the breaking of our lines near Petersburg,
and with this a full comprehension of the fact that
the days of the Confederacy were numbered. I
was in Richmond on Sunday, April 2, and escorted
to church a young lady whose looks and apparel
were in perfect keeping with the beautiful spring
day. The green-checked silk dress she wore looked
as fresh and unspotted as if it had just run the
blockade. As the church we attended was not the
one at which the news of the disaster had been
handed to President Davis, our services were not
interrupted, nor did I hear anything of it until I
had parted with her at her home and gone to the
house of a relative, Dr. Randolph Page's, to dine.
There I learned that a fierce battle had been fought
at Five Forks, on the extreme right of our line, in
which the Federals had gotten possession of the
railroads by which our army was supplied with food.
This, of course, necessitated the abandonment of
both Richmond and Petersburg.

As I passed along the streets in the afternoon

there was nothing to indicate a panicky feeling; in fact, there was rather less commotion than usual, but much, no doubt, within doors.

On arriving at camp I was the first to bring tidings of what had occurred to the company, and observed the varying effect produced on the different members, officers and men. To some it came as relief after long suspense, while others seemed hopelessly cast down and dejected. Orders to prepare to move soon followed, and our march to and through Richmond began with only two of our four guns, the other two being left behind for want of horses.

We reached the city shortly before midnight, and, with Estill Waddell, of our battalion, I passed by the home of some friends, who, we found, had retired for the night. In response to my call, the head of the house appeared at an upper window. I had with me the few valuables I possessed, among them the brass button worn on my jacket and indented by the shell at second Cold Harbor. These I tossed into the yard, with the request that he would keep them for me. And, some months after the war, the package was sent to me in Lexington.

We could now see and realize what the evacuation of Richmond involved. Waddell had learned that his brother James, adjutant of the Twenty-fourth Virginia Infantry, had been wounded the day before at Petersburg, and was in the Chimborazo Hospital. At this we soon arrived, and entered a large apartment with low ceiling and brilliantly lighted. On row after row of cots lay wounded men, utterly oblivious and indifferent to the serious conditions that disturbed those of us who realized what they were. Nurses and attendants were extremely scarce, and as deep silence prevailed as if each cot contained a corpse.

After a search of a few moments Waddell recognized his brother in sound sleep. His appearance for manly beauty, as we stood over him, surpassed that of any figure I have ever seen. His slight, graceful form stretched at full length, a snow-white forehead fringed with dark hair, and chin resting on his chest, he lay like an artist's model rather than a wounded warrior, and the smile with which his brown eyes opened at the sound of his brother's voice betokened the awakening from a dream of peace and home. On another cot, a few steps farther on, I recognized John McClintic, of the Rockbridge Cavalry, and brother of my messmate. He was a boy of seventeen, with his arm shattered at the shoulder. On the cot next to him lay a man who was dying. McClintic and the others near him who could make their wants known were almost famished for water, a bucket of which, after much difficulty, we secured for them. On the following day this young fellow, rather than be left in the hands of the Federals, rode in an ox-cart and walked twenty miles, and finally reached his home in Rockbridge.

After leaving the hospital we passed on to Main street and the business part of the city, where the scene would remind one of Bulwer's description of "The Last Days of Pompeii." The storehouses had been broken into and stood wide open, and fires had been kindled out of the goods boxes, on the floors, to afford light to plunder. Articles of liquid nature, especially intoxicants, had been emptied into the gutters, from which such portions as could be rescued were being greedily sought.

From dark garrets and cellars the old hags and half-starved younger women and children had gathered, and were reaping a harvest such as they had never dreamed of. I saw a small boy, with an old, wrinkled, grinning woman at his heels, steer a barrel of flour around a corner and into a narrow alley with the speed and skill of a roustabout. The fire on the floors had not extended to the structures as we passed, but as no one seemed in the least concerned or interfered with their progress the flames soon put in their work and spread in all directions.

We crossed the James on Mayo's Bridge, following the road in a southwesterly direction. With the first appearance of dawn the blowing up of the naval vessels in the river began, culminating in a gigantic explosion that made the earth tremble. This last was the magazine at Drewry's Bluff.

Witnessing such scenes, with a realization of their significance, in the early part of our war experience would, no doubt, have been hopelessly demoralizing, but now the calmness and fortitude with which we took it demonstrated the fact that four years of such schooling had seasoned us to meet unflinchingly the most desperate situations. When broad daylight came we had the opportunity of seeing some of the heterogeneous elements of which Richmond was composed.   Disaster had come too suddenly to afford time beforehand for the non-combatants to migrate, even if there had been safe places to which to flee.

That such looking objects should have undertaken to accompany an army in the field, or rather into the fields, indicated what desperate chances they were willing to take rather than abandon themselves to a doubtful fate by remaining behind. In addition to the city contingent and those who garrisoned the forts where heavy ordnance only was used, the line of march was joined by the marine department, which had been doing duty on the river craft about Dutch Gap, Drewry's and Chaffin's bluffs, etc.   Altogether, it was a motley combination, which afforded much amusement and the usual sallies of wit at each other's expense.   The marine element was the most striking in appearance, and encumbered with enough baggage for a voyage to the North Pole.   In three days' time this had all been discarded.

After marching day and night the two wings of our army, having been separated since the previous summer, united at Amelia Court House, about 40 miles from Richmond. Ours—that is, the one from the north side of the river—had not been pressed by the enemy up to this point. As if in recognition of and to celebrate the reunion, an explosion took place far too violent for an ordinary salute. During a short halt, while the road was filled with infantry and artillery side by side, we felt the earth heave under our feet, followed instantly by a terrific report, and then a body of fire and flame, a hundred feet in diameter, shot skyward from beyond an intervening copse of woods. It proved to be the blowing up of sixty caissons, one hundred and eighty chests of ammunition, which could not be hauled farther for want of horses. For a moment the roar and concussion produced consternation. Those who were standing crouched as if for something to cling to, and those sitting sprang to their feet. The Crater affair at Petersburg had not been forgotten, and that we should be hurled into space by some infernal eruption flashed into our minds.

Provisions had been ordered by General Lee over the railroad from Danville to Amelia Court House in readiness for the army on its arrival there. By some misunderstanding, or negligence on the part of the railroad management, these supplies had gone on to Richmond, so that all expectation of satisfying hunger was now gone. Corn on the cob had already been issued to the men, which, it may be presumed, was to be eaten raw, as no time nor means for parching it was available. Three of these "nubbins," which had been preserved, I saw many years after the war.

After trudging along, with short halts and making very little progress, our battery of only two guns went into park about midnight, but without unhitching the horses. After being roused several times from sleep to march, I concluded, after the third false alarm, to lie still. When I awoke some time later the battery had moved and, in the dim light, I failed to find the course it had taken. Folfowing on for some distance I came to General Lee's headquarters in a farmhouse by the roadside, and was informed by Capt. James Garnett, one of the staff, that the battery would soon pass along the road at the point we then were. Sitting down with my back against a tree I, of course, fell asleep. From this I was shortly roused by rapid firing close by, and saw our wagon-train scattered and fleeing across the fields, with horses at a run and hotly pursued by Federal cavalry, who, with reins on their horses' necks, were firing at them with repeating guns. I was overlooked and passed by in the chase as too small game for them.

The road over which I had passed was in the form of a semi-circle, and to escape I obliqued across the fields to a point I had gone over an hour or two before, where it crossed Sailor's Creek. Along the road, ascending the hill on the south side of the creek, I found several brigades of our infantry, commanded by Ex-Governor Billy Smith, Gen. Custis Lee and Colonel Crutchfield, halted in the road and exposed to a sharp artillery fire, which, notwithstanding the fact that the place was heavily wooded, was very accurate and searching. Colonel Crutchfield was killed here, his head being taken off by a solid shot. This was not a comfortable place in which to linger while waiting for the battery, but comfortable places in that neighborhood seemed exceedingly scarce.

Very soon my friend, Henry Wise, who was a lieutenant in Huger's battalion of artillery, appeared on horseback and informed me that almost all of the cannoneers of his battalion had just been captured and that he was then in search of men to take their places. I offered my services, and, following the directions he gave, soon found his guns, and was assigned to a number at one of them by Lieut. George Poindexter, another old acquaintance of Lexington.

The infantry at this part of the line was what was left of Pickett's division, among whom I recognized and chatted with other old friends of the Virginia Military Institute as we sat resignedly waiting for the impending storm to burst. The Federal cavalry which had passed me previously in pursuit of our wagons, quartermasters, etc., was part of a squadron that had gotten in rear of Pickett's men and given General Pickett and staff a hot chase for some distance along the line of his command. Some of their men and horses were killed in their eagerness to overhaul the General. It was perfectly evident that our thin line of battle was soon to be assaulted, as the enemy's skirmishers were advancing on our front and right flank and his cannon sweeping the position from our left. We were not long in suspense. Almost simultaneously we were raked by missiles from three directions. To have offered resistance would have been sheer folly. In fifteen minutes the few survivors of Pickett's immortal division had been run over and captured, together with the brigades which were posted on their left.

Lieutenant Wise having failed to receive any other cannoneers to replace those previously captured, the guns, without firing a shot, were left standing unlimbered. As we started in haste to retire, he and Poindexter being mounted, expressed great concern lest I, being on foot, should be captured. Just as they left me, however, and while the air seemed filled with flying lead and iron, I came upon one of the ambulance corps who was trying to lead an unruly horse. It was a Federal cavalry horse, whose rider had been killed in pursuit of General Pickett. In the horse's efforts to break loose, the two saddles he was carrying had slipped from his back and were dangling underneath, which increased his fright. I suggested to the man that, to escape capture, he had better give me the horse, as he seemed to be afraid to ride him. To this he readily assented, and, with his knife, cut one saddle loose, set the other on his back, and handed me the halter-strap as I mounted. The terrified animal, without bridle or spur, was off like a flash, and in a few minutes had carried me out of the mêlée. I still have and prize the saddle. The few who escaped from this affair, known as the battle of Sailor's Creek, by retreating a mile north came in proximity to another column of our troops marching on a parallel road.

As I rode up I saw General Lee dismounted and standing on a railroad embankment, intently observing our fleeing men, who now began to throng about him. He very quietly but firmly let them know that it would be best not to collect in groups; the importance of which they at once understood and acted on.

Approaching night, which on previous occasions, when conditions were reversed, had interfered to our disadvantage, now shielded us from further pursuit. It can readily be seen what demoralization would follow such an exhibition of our utter helplessness. But still there seemed to be no alternative but to prolong the agony, although perfectly assured that we could not escape death or capture, and that in a very brief time. Soon after nightfall I found our battery, which had traveled over a shorter and less exposed road, and thereby escaped the adventures which had fallen to my lot. Our course was now toward High Bridge, which spans the Appomattox River near Farmville. On we toiled throughout the night, making very slow progress, but not halting until near noon the following day. Under present conditions there were not the ordinary inducements to make a halt, as food for man and beast was not in evidence. I had not eaten a bite for forty-eight hours. Notwithstanding this, and as if to draw attention from our empty stomachs, orders came to countermarch and meet a threatened attack on the line in our rear. To this the two guns with their detachments promptly responded, reported to General Mahone and took part with his division in a spirited battle at Cumberland Church.

It has been stated, by those who had opportunities of knowing, that Mahone's division was never driven from its position in battle throughout the four years of the war. True or not, it held good in this case, and those of our battery who took part with them were enthusiastic over the gallant fight they made under circumstances that were not inspiring. There being a surplus of men to man our two guns, Lieut. Cole Davis and Billy McCauley procured muskets and took part with the infantry sharpshooters. McCauley was killed. He was a model soldier, active and wiry as a cat and tough as a hickory sapling. He had seen infantry service before joining our battery, and, as already mentioned, had "rammed home" one hundred and sev-

Launcelot Minor

enty-five shells in the first battle of Fredericksburg. Another member of our company, Launcelot Minor, a boy of less than eighteen years, was shot through the lungs by a Minie-ball. He was thought to be dying, but was carried from the field, as he tells in the following extract from a letter recently received from him: "I am almost too old to begin to write a history of myself, but will try to give you an account of things from April 8th, 1865, to August, 1865, when I got back to my home in Albemarle County, Virginia. After the line was formed at Cumberland Church, and after we had extricated ourselves from the swamps at High Bridge, I was sent to burn the remaining wagons, but was soon ordered to the battery, which was in action on the hill. About three or four o'clock that evening I was shot and was taken by Bumpus and Ruffin to a blacksmith-shop some distance away. I was in my right mind for several hours and remember that many came to tell me good-by as they left the field. Old Byrd, I remember well, and Bumpus asking him if he could do anything, and Byrd said, 'You dig a hole and he will be ready for it by the time it is done.'

"The next thing I knew it was April 18th, and I found myself on a mattress in the house of a Mrs. Hobson, and a dead Yankee by my side. My clothes had not been moved, but an angel woman, Miss Hobson, was sticking a spoon of chicken broth into my mouth. I wish I could describe this woman—

for I had been dead and associated with the Heavenly Host, and thought one had followed me to earth. She told me that the dead Yankee had taken from my breast the note and fifty cents that Bumpus had put there and replaced it with five dollars in gold; this was done, she said, the morning I 'came to' and he died. At the Louisville Reunion, Bumpus, whom I saw for the first time since the war, told me that he had written the note and placed fifty cents in it, and it requested that 'whoever may find this body will please notify Mrs. Dr. Charles Minor, at Charlottesville, Virginia, and mark the grave and accept in token this fifty cents.' The note was intact when I came to myself, but instead of fifty cents it contained five dollars in gold, which did valuable service in those trying times. When I got home, in the latter part of August, 1865, I found my mother and sisters destitute, and brother Charles working to keep things alive—no cow, no horses—only an old blind ox, not fit for beef and too poor to die. I have inquired diligently for the good woman who nursed me to life, but could never learn anything of her nor of my Yankee friend."

CHAPTER XXIX

APPOMATTOX

ANOTHER night was now at hand, and while it might be supposed that nothing could be added to intensify the suspense there certainly was nothing to allay it. Although there was little left to destroy, we passed heaps of burning papers, abandoned wagons, etc., along the roadsides.

As each new scene or condition in our lives gives rise to some new and corresponding feeling or emotion, our environment at this time was such as to evoke sensations of dread and apprehension hitherto unknown. Moving parallel with us, and extending its folds like some huge reptile, was an army equipped with the best the world could afford—threefold greater in numbers than our own—which in four years had never succeeded in defeating us in a general battle, but which we had repeatedly routed and driven to cover. Impatient of delay in effecting our overthrow in battle, in order to starve us out, marauding bands had scoured the country, leaving ashes and desolation in their wake.

That now their opportunity to pay up old scores had come, we fully realized, and anticipated with dread the day of reckoning. General Grant, who was Commander-in-Chief of all the Federal armies, and at present personally in command of the army about us, was by no means regarded as a man of mercy. He had positively refused to exchange prisoners, thousands of whom on both sides were languishing and dying in the hands of their captors. It should be borne in mind, in this connection, that the offers to exchange had come from the Confederate authorities, and for the last two years of the war had been invariably rejected by the Federal Government. In the campaign beginning in May, 1864, and ending with the evacuation of Richmond, Grant's army had sustained a loss greater in number than that of the whole army opposed to him.

Among the ranks were foreigners of every nationality. I had seen, as prisoners in our hands, a whole brigade of Germans who could not speak a word of English. During the preceding winter we had been confronted with regiments of our former slaves. Our homes and people we were leaving behind to the mercy of these hordes, as if forever.

Another and by no means unimportant consideration was whether to remain and meet results with the command, or for each man to shift for himself. Setting out from Richmond on the preceding Sunday, with no accumulation of vigor to draw on, we had passed a week with food and sleep scarcely sufficient for one day; and to cope with such exigencies as now confronted us, what a part the stomach does play! All in all, it was a situation of a lifetime that will ever abide in the gloomy recesses of memory. About eight o'clock on Sunday morning, April 9, as our two guns were entering the little village of Appomattox, several cannonshots sounded in quick succession immediately in our front. Without word of command we came to our last halt.

Turning out of the road we went into park, unhitched our hungry horses, and awaited developments. During the two preceding days several written communications had passed between Generals Lee and Grant, of which we knew nothing. Our suspense, however, was soon interrupted by the appearance of a Confederate officer, accompanied by a Federal officer with long, flowing yellow hair, and waving a white handkerchief as they galloped by. This was General Custer, of cavalry fame, and the conspicuous hero and victim of the Indian massacre, which bore his name, in Montana ten years later.

Several sharp encounters had occurred during the morning, in which our men displayed the same unflinching valor, capturing in a charge a Federal major-general (Gregg) and two pieces of artillery; but now all firing had ceased, and the stillness that followed was oppressive. As soon as it became known that General Lee had surrendered, although for days it had been perfectly understood that such a result was inevitable, there was for a time no little excitement and commotion among the men. That we should be subjected to abhorrent humiliation was conceived as a matter of course, and, to avoid it, all sorts of efforts and plans to escape were discussed. The one controlling influence, however, to allay such a feeling was the unbounded and unimpaired confidence in General Lee. The conduct and bearing of the men were characterized by the same sterling qualities they had always displayed. The only exhibition of petulance that I witnessed was by a staff officer who bore no scars or other evidence of hardships undergone, but who acquired great reputation after the war. He "could not submit to such degradation," etc., threw away his spurs and chafed quite dramatically. When a bystander suggested that we cut our way out, he objected that we had no arms. "We can follow those that have." was the reply, "and use the guns of those that fall!" He did not accede to the proposition; but later I heard him insist that one of our drivers should let him have his spurs, as he, the driver, would have no further use for them; but he did not get the spurs.

By noon, or soon thereafter, the terms of the surrender were made known—terms so generous, considerate, and unlooked-for as scarcely believed to be possible. None of that exposure to the gaze and exultation of a victorious foe, such as we had seen pictured in our schoolbooks, or as practised by conquering nations in all times. We had felt it as not improbable that, after an ordeal of mortifying exposure for the gratification of the military, we would be paraded through Northern cities for the benefit of jeering crowds. So, when we learned that we should be paroled, and go to our homes unmolested, the relief was unbounded.

Early in the afternoon General Lee, mounted on "Traveler" and clad in a spotless new uniform, passed along on his return from an interview with General Grant. I stood close by the roadside, along which many of his old soldiers had gathered, in anticipation of his coming, and, in a life of more than three-score years, with perhaps more than ordinary opportunities of seeing inspiring sights, both of God's and man's creation, the impression and effect of General Lee's face and appearance as he rode by, hat in hand, stands pre-eminent. A few of the men started to cheer, but almost instantly ceased, and stood in silence with the others—all with heads bared.

The favorable and entirely unexpected terms of surrender wonderfully restored our souls; and at once plans, first for returning to our homes, and then for starting life anew, afforded ample interest and entertainment. One of the privileges granted in the terms of surrender was the retention, by officers and cavalrymen, of their own horses. My recent acquisition at Sailor's Creek had put me in possession of a horse, but to retain him was the difficulty, as I was neither officer nor cavalryman. Buoyed up with the excitement of bursting shells and the noise of battle, he had carried me out gamely, but, this over, there was little life in him. I transferred the saddle and bridle to a horse abandoned in the road with some artillery, and left my old benefactor standing, with limbs wide apart and head down.

To accomplish my purpose of going out with a horse, two obstacles had first to be overcome. Being only a cannoneer, I was not supposed to own a horse, so I must be something else. I laid the case before General Pendleton, our old neighbor in Lexington, and my former school-teacher. It was rather late to give me a commission, but he at once appointed me a courier on his staff, and as such I was paroled, and still have the valued little paper, a *facsimile* of which is shown opposite.

The next difficulty to be met, the horse I had exchanged for was branded C.S., and, even if allowed to pass then, I feared would be confiscated later. There was a handsome sorrel, also branded C.S., among our battery horses, to which Lieut. Ned Dandridge, of General Pendleton's staff, had taken a fancy. For the sorrel he substituted a big, bony young bay of his own. I replaced the bay with my C.S. horse, and was now equipped for peace. The branded sorrel was soon taken by the Federals.

The final parting of a body of men associated as we had been through the trying years of what had seemed an interminable war, after having endured all things as we thought; having together enjoyed

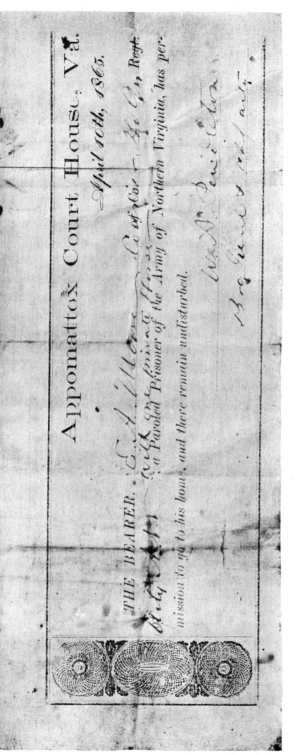

FAC-SIMILE OF PAROLE SIGNED BY GENERAL PENDLETON

to the utmost the gaiety in camp and on the march, the quick wit, the jolly jest with sharp repartee, the mad rush through our border towns on the heels of the fleeing invaders, with the women and children wild with delight and gratitude; the sight of the mighty forces marshalling, preliminary to battle; the music of the bands; the return from prison of companions whose fate was unknown; some of us to set out for homes comparatively near, some to those more or less remote; others to homes amid hostile surroundings, others again whose homes had been destroyed and loved ones scattered, while there stood around us the starving horses, our familiar and faithful friends, still tied to the guns in mute dejection—was an experience not to be undergone unmoved. But buoyed with the consciousness that we had fought a good fight, continuing even after our faith was finished, under two commanders to whom in military skill, in nobility of character, and in purity of life, the rest of the world has produced no equal; and last but not least, that the cause for which we had undergone it all was not one we *thought* was right but that we *knew* was right. With associations such as these, and attachments the depth of which was realized only in later years, each to every other said "good-by," and on the 11th a party, consisting of Col. Edmund Pendleton of the Eighth Louisiana Regiment (whose family resided in an adjoining county), Lieut.-Col. W. T. Poague, of

A. P. Hill's Artillery; Lieut. Jack Jordan, Sergt. John McCauley, Private James Lewis, and myself, of the Rockbridge Artillery, all mounted took the road leading home, occasionally encountering a Federal officer, attended by an orderly who passed us in silence. From Canal street at Lynchburg, along which we rode, could be seen the quiet streets ascending from the river, all dreary and silent, with a blue-coat here and there holding sway. Thence across the James by a bridge into Amherst, where we spent the night at two farm-houses and were most hospitably and generously entertained. At Balcony Falls our routes diverged, one after another taking a straight course home. For months after I reached Lexington, on the 14th, from every quarter, singly and in pairs, others came as time permitted, after the various detached commands had laid down their arms or Northern prisons discharged their emaciated inmates. The scarcity of food in the community was supplemented with rations issued from a Federal commissary in our town until gardens and truck-patches could be made available.

After resting and fattening my bay, I sold him for a good price, and was thus enabled to return to Washington College and serve again under General Lee.

APPENDIX

UNDER an act of the General Assembly of Virginia, 1898, the Camps of Confederate Veterans, organized in the several cities and towns of the Commonwealth, were authorized to prepare lists of the citizens of their respective counties who served as soldiers during the war between the States, and of those belonging to such companies, and these lists were to be duly recorded by the Clerks of the County Courts of the counties and kept among the Court Records. The following list is taken from this record, and is as nearly accurate as is possible at this date:

ROCKBRIDGE ARTILLERY

ROLL OF COMPANY

THE enrollment of the Rockbridge Artillery began April 19, 1861, and by the 21st the company numbered about seventy men, and was organized by the election of the following officers: Captain, John McCausland; and J. Bowyer Brockenbrough, Wm. McLaughlin and Wm. T. Poague, lieutenants. Captain McCausland soon thereafter was made lieutenant-colonel and ordered to the western part of the State. On the 29th of April the company unanimously elected Rev. Wm. N. Pendleton captain.

The company left Lexington for the seat of war May 10, 1861, with two small, brass six-pounders obtained at the Virginia Military Institute. It was regularly mustered into the Confederate service at Staunton, Virginia, on May 11, and at once ordered to Harper's Ferry, where it received two more guns. After the First Brigade was organized, under Gen. Thomas J. Jackson, the Rockbridge Artillery was assigned to it, and continued a component part of the Stonewall Brigade, in touch with and occupying the same positions with it in all its battles and skirmishes up to Sharpsburg.

Upon the reorganization of the artillery, in October, 1862, the battery was assigned to the First Regiment Virginia Artillery, under the command of Col. J. Thompson Brown, and continued with it till the close of the war. The first fight it was engaged in, and which made a part of its history, occurred July 2 near Hainesville, when General Patterson crossed the Potomac and advanced on Winchester. But one piece was engaged, and this fired the first shot from a Confederate gun in the Shenandoah Valley.

The battery had five captains from first to last: First, John McCausland, afterward brigadier-general of cavalry; second, Rev. Wm. N. Pendleton, D.D., in command from May 1, 1861, until after the first battle of Manassas, afterward brigadier-general and chief of artillery in the Army of Northern Virginia; third, Wm. McLaughlin, afterward lieutenant-colonel of artillery, in command until April 2, 1862; fourth, Wm. T. Poague, afterward lieutenant-colonel of artillery, Army of Northern Virginia, in command until after the first battle of Fredericksburg; fifth, Archibald Graham, from that time until the surrender at Appomattox, at which place ninety-three men and officers laid down their arms.

This company had the reputation of being one of the finest companies in the service. So high was the intellectual quality of the men that forty-five were commissioned as officers and assigned to other companies in the service. Many of them reached high distinction. At no time during the war did this company want for recruits, but it was so popular that it always had a list from which it could fill its ranks, which were sometimes depleted by its heavy casualties and numerous promotions from its roster.

The following officers and men were mustered into the service of the Confederate States at Staunton, Virginia, on the 11th day of May, 1861:

*Captain W. N. Pendleton; brigadier-general, chief of artillery A.N.V.; paroled at Appomattox.

The names with a star prefixed are the men from Rockbridge County.

*First Lieutenant J. B. Brockenbrough; wounded at first Manassas; captain Baltimore Artillery, major of artillery A.N.V.

*Second Lieutenant Wm. McLaughlin; captain; lieutenant-colonel of artillery.

*Second Lieutenant W. T. Poague; captain; lieutenant-colonel of artillery A.N.V.; wounded at second Cold Harbor; paroled at Appomattox.

*First Sergeant J. McD. Alexander; lieutenant Rockbridge Artillery; entered cavalry.

*Second Sergeant J. Cole Davis; lieutenant Rockbridge Artillery; wounded at Port Republic; paroled at Appomattox.

*Third Sergeant Archibald Graham; lieutenant and captain Rockbridge Artillery; paroled at Appomattox.

PRIVATES

*Agnor, Jos. S.; killed at Fredericksburg December 13, 1862.

*Ayres, Jas.; discharged for physical disability August, 1861.

*Ayres, N. B.; deserted, went into Federal army.

*Anderson, S. D.; killed at Kernstown March 23, 1862.

*Beard, John; killed at Fredericksburg December 13, 1862.

*Beard, W. B.; died from effects of measles summer of 1861.

*Bain, Samuel.

*Brockenbrough, W. N.; corporal; transferred to Baltimore Light Artillery.

*Brown, W. M.; corporal, sergeant, lieutenant; wounded and captured at Gettysburg.

*Bumpus, W. N.; corporal; paroled at Appomattox.

*Conner, Blain; discharged for physical disability in spring, 1861.

*Conner, George; arm broken by stallion; absent after winter of 1861-62.

*Conner, Jas. A.; wounded at Sharpsburg and Gettysburg; took the oath in prison and joined Federal army and fought Indians in Northwest.

*Conner, John C.; paroled at Appomattox.

*Coffee, A. W.

*Craig, John B.; paroled at Appomattox.

*Crosen, W.

*Curran, Daniel; died from disease in summer of 1862.

*Davis, Mark; deserted.

*Davis, R. G.; died from disease in 1861.

*Doran, John; wounded at Malvern Hill in 1862; disabled.

*Dudley, R. M.

*Ford, Henry; discharged after one year.

*Ford, Jas. A.; wounded.

*Gibbs, J. T., Jr.; wounded at Port Republic June 22, 1862; died from disease.

*Gold, J. M.; captured at Gettysburg and died in prison.

*Gordon, W. C.; wounded at Fredericksburg; disabled.

*Harris, Alex.; captured at Gettysburg and died in prison.

*Harris, Bowlin; captured at Gettysburg; kept in prison.

*Hetterick, Ferdinand; discharged after one year.

*Henry, N. S.; corporal, sergeant; paroled at Appomattox.

*Hughes, Wm.; discharged.

*Hostetter, G. W.; transferred to infantry.

*Johnson, Lawson; died in summer of 1861.

*Johnson, W. F.; corporal, quartermaster sergeant; paroled at Appomattox.

*Jordan, J. W.; wounded at first Manassas; corporal, sergeant, lieutenant; paroled at Appomattox.

*Leopard, Jas.; transferred to Carpenter's battery.

*Lewis, Henry P.; paroled at Appomattox.

*Lewis, R. P.; transferred to cavalry in spring of 1862.

*Leyburn, John; lieutenant Rockbridge Artillery; surgeon on privateer.

*Martin, Thomas; wounded and captured at Gettysburg.

*McCampbell, D. A.; died from disease in December, 1864.

*McCampbell, W. H.; paroled at Appomattox.

*McCluer, John G.; corporal Rockbridge Artillery; transferred to cavalry.

*McCorkle, J. Baxter; corporal, sergeant, lieutenant Rockbridge Artillery; killed at first Fredericksburg.

*Montgomery, W. G.; killed at first Fredericksburg.

*Moore, D. E.; corporal, sergeant; wounded at Winchester and at Malvern Hill; paroled at Appomattox.

*Moore, John D.; quartermaster sergeant; captured after Gettysburg, prisoner until close of war.

*Moore, Samuel R.; mortally wounded at Sharpsburg.

*Morgan, G. W.; sick and absent most of the time.

*O'Rourke, Frank; wounded at Malvern Hill; deserted.

*Paxton, J. Lewis; sergeant; lost leg at Kernstown.

*Phillips, James.

*Preston, Frank; lost an arm at Winchester May 25, 1862; captain Virginia Military Institute Company.

*Raynes, A. G.; detailed as miller.

*Rader, D. P.; wounded at Fredericksburg December 13, 1862.

*Rhodes, J. N.; discharged, over age.

*Smith, Joseph S.; transferred to cavalry; killed in battle.

*Smith, S. C.; corporal, sergeant; paroled at Appomattox.

*Smith, Adam; discharged after one year.

*Strickler, James.

*Strickler, W. L.; corporal, sergeant; paroled at Appomattox.

*Silvey, James; paroled at Appomattox.

*Tharp, Benjamin F.; transferred to cavalry in spring of 1862.

*Thompson, John A.; paroled at Appomattox.

*Thompson, S. G.

*Tompkins, J. F.; corporal; detailed in Ordnance Department.

*Trevy, Jacob; wounded at Gettysburg; paroled at Appomattox.

*Wallace, John; killed at Kernstown March 23, 1862.

*Wilson, S. A.; discharged for physical disability August, 1861; joined cavalry.

The following joined the battery after May 11, 1861; dates of enlistment being given as far as known:

*Adams, Thomas T.; enlisted 1863; discharged; later killed in battle.

*Adkins, Blackburn; paroled at Appomattox.

*Agnor, Oscar W.; paroled at Appomattox.

*Agnor, John; enlisted July 21, 1861.

*Agnor, Jonathan; enlisted July 29, 1861; killed at Kernstown May 25, 1862.

*Agnor, Samuel S.; enlisted fall of 1862.

Alexander, Edgar S.; enlisted September 2, 1861; lost an arm at Fredericksburg, 1862.

Alexander, Eugene, enlisted August 23, 1861; wounded at second Manassas; transferred to cavalry.

Armisted, Charles J.; paroled at Appomattox.

Arnold, A. E.; enlisted September 1, 1861; corporal, assistant surgeon.

Bacon, Edloe P.; paroled at Appomattox.

Bacon, Edloe P., Jr.; paroled at Appomattox.

Baldwin, William Ludwell, paroled at Appomattox.

Barger, William G.; paroled at Appomattox.

Barton, David R.; enlisted June 27, 1861; lieutenant in Cutshaw's battery; killed.

Barton, Robert T.; enlisted March 7, 1862.

Bedinger, G. R.; July 9, 1861; transferred to infantry; killed at Gettysburg; captain.

Bealle, Jerry T.; enlisted November 21, 1861.

Bell, Robert S.; enlisted November 19, 1861; killed at Rappahannock Station.

*Black, Benjamin F.; paroled at Appomattox.

Blain, Daniel; enlisted May 27, 1861; detailed in Ordnance Department; paroled at Appomattox.

Blackford, L. M.; enlisted September 2, 1861; adjutant Twenty-sixth Virginia Infantry.

Bolling, W. H.; enlisted March 10, 1862; corporal.

Boteler, A. R., Jr.; enlisted March 1, 1862; wounded May 25, 1862.

Boteler, Charles P.; enlisted October 23, 1861; transferred to cavalry.

Boteler, Henry; enlisted October 10, 1861 ; corporal; paroled at Appomattox.

Boyd, E. Holmes; enlisted June 28, 1861; transferred to Ordnance Department.

Brooke, Pendleton; enlisted October 28, 1861; discharged for physical disability.

Brown, H. C.; enlisted 1862; detailed in Signal Corps.

*Brown, John L.; enlisted July 23, 1861; killed at Malvern Hill.

Brown, John M.; enlisted March 11, 1862; wounded at Malvern Hill; paroled at Appomattox.

Bryan, Edward; enlisted November 22, 1861.

Burwell, Lewis P.; enlisted September 21, 1861; transferred.

Byers, G. Newton; enlisted August 23, 1861; corporal; paroled at Appomattox.

*Byrd, W. H.; enlisted August 15, 1861; killed at Kernstown March 23, 1862.

*Byrd, William.

*Carson, William; enlisted July 23, 1861; corporal; paroled at Appomattox.

Caruthers, Thornton; enlisted December 21, 1862.

*Chapin, W. T.

Clark, James G.; enlisted June 15, 1861; transferred.

Clark, J. Gregory; enlisted July 16, 1862; transferred.

Cook, Richard D.; paroled at Appomattox.

*Compton, Robert K.; enlisted July 25, 1861; paroled at Appomattox.

*Conner, Alexander; enlisted July 23, 1861; wounded May 25, 1862, at Winchester; paroled at Appomattox.

*Conner, Daniel; enlisted July 27, 1862.

*Conner, Fitz G.

*Conner, Henry C.; paroled at Appomattox.

*Cox, W. H.; enlisted July 23, 1861.

*Craig, Joseph E.; enlisted March 2, 1863.

*Crocken, Francis J.; enlisted March 21, 1862.

Dandridge, A. Stephen; enlisted 1862; paroled at Appomattox.

Darnall, Andrew M.; captured at Deep Bottom.

Darnall, Henry T.; enlisted July 23, 1861; paroled at Appomattox.

*Davis, Charles W.; paroled at Appomattox.

Davis, James M. M.; paroled at Appomattox.

*Davis, John E.; died from disease June, 1864.

*Dixon, W. H. H.; enlisted July 23, 1861; wounded December 13, 1862; paroled at Appomattox.

*Dold, C. M.; enlisted March 3, 1862; wounded at Newtown; paroled at Appomattox.

Effinger, W. H.; wounded at Sharpsburg; transferred to engineers.

Emmett, Michael J.; enlisted June 15, 1861; wounded and captured at Gettysburg.

Eppes, W. H.; wounded September, 1862.

*Estill, W. C.; paroled at Appomattox.

Fairfax, Randolph; enlisted August 10, 1861; wounded at Malvern Hill; killed at first Fredericksburg.

Faulkner, E. Boyd; enlisted July 23, 1862; detailed at headquarters.

Fishburne, C. D.; enlisted June 21, 1861; sergeant; lieutenant in Ordnance Department.

Foutz, Henry; enlisted September 6, 1862; killed at first Fredericksburg.

Frazer, Robert; enlisted November 28, 1862; wounded at first Fredericksburg.

Friend, Ben C. M.; paroled at Appomattox.

*Fuller, John; enlisted July 23, 1861; wounded at Malvern Hill; killed at first Fredericksburg.

Garnett, James M.; enlisted July 17, 1861; lieutenant on staff; captain in Ordnance Department; paroled at Appomattox.

Gibson, Henry B.; enlisted May 13, 1862.

Gibson, John T.; enlisted August 14, 1861.

Gibson, Robert A.; paroled at Appomattox.

Gilliam, William T.

Gilmer, James B.; paroled at Appomattox.

*Gilmore, J. Harvey; enlisted March 7, 1862; chaplain.

*Ginger, George A.; enlisted March 6, 1862; wounded at Newtown; paroled at Appomattox.

*Ginger, W. L.; enlisted March 6, 1862; wounded and captured at Gettysburg; prisoner till close of war.

*Gold, Alfred; enlisted July 23, 1861; wounded at second Fredericksburg.

Gooch, James T.; transferred from engineers in 1863; paroled at Appomattox.

*Guul, John M.; enlisted June 14, 1861; chaplain A.N.V.; died of fever in service.

*Gray, O. P.; enlisted March 21, 1862; killed at Kernstown March 23, 1862.

Gregory, John M.; enlisted September 7, 1861; wounded May 25, 1862; captain in Ordnance Department.

*Green, Thomas; enlisted 1862; transferred.

*Green, Zach.; enlisted 1862; transferred.

Gross, Charles; enlisted July 27, 1862.

*Hall, John F.; enlisted July 23, 1861; died near Richmond, 1862.

Heiskell, J. Campbell; enlisted February 9, 1862; wounded in 1864; paroled at Appomattox.

Heiskell, J. P.; enlisted 1862; discharged for physical disability.

*Herndon, Francis T.; enlisted March 31, 1862; killed at Malvern Hill.

Hitner, John K.; enlisted March 17, 1862; wounded.

*Holmes, John A.; enlisted March 11, 1862.

*Houston, James Rutherford; enlisted July 23, 1861.

Houston, William W.; enlisted August 10, 1861; chaplain A.N.V.

Hughes, William; enlisted July 23, 1861.

Hummerickhouse, John R.; enlisted March 28, 1862.

Hyde, Edward H.; enlisted March 28, 1862; paroled at Appomattox.

Johnson, Thomas E.

Jones, Beverly R.; enlisted July 3, 1861.

Kean, Otho G.; enlisted after capture at Vicksburg; paroled at Appomattox.

Kean, William C.; enlisted fall of 1861; transferred.

*Knick, William; enlisted August 11, 1862; mortally wounded at second Fredericksburg.

Lacy, Richard B.

Lacy, William S.; enlisted March 17, 1862; detailed in Signal Service; chaplain.

Lawson, Joseph; enlisted July 20, 1863.

Lawson, William; enlisted July 20, 1863.

Leathers, John P.; paroled at Appomattox.

*Lecky, John H.; enlisted July 23, 1861; transferred to cavalry.

Lee, Robert E., Jr.; enlisted March 26, 1862; lieutenant on staff, and captain.

*Leech, James M.; paroled at Appomattox.

*Letcher, Samuel H.; paroled at Appomattox.

*Lewis, James P.; enlisted July 23, 1861; wounded.

Lewis, Nicholas H.; enlisted June 17, 1861.

*Link, David; transferred from Rice's battery.

Luke, Williamson; enlisted October 7, 1861; soon transferred to cavalry.

*McAlpin, Joseph; enlisted March 3, 1862; mortally wounded at first Fredericksburg.

*McCauley, John E.; enlisted July 23, 1861; corporal, sergeant; paroled at Appomattox.

*McCauley, William H.; transferred from infantry; corporal; killed April 7, 1865.

*McClintic, W. S.; enlisted October 4, 1861; wounded; paroled at Appomattox.

*McCorkle, Tazwell E.; enlisted in Hampden-Sidney Company in 1861; captured at Rich Mountain; joined battery in 1864.

*McCorkle, Thomas E.; enlisted March 9, 1862; paroled at Appomattox.

*McCorkle, William A.; enlisted July 23, 1861; paroled at Appomattox.

*McCrum, R. Barton; paroled at Appomattox.

McGuire, Hugh H., Jr.; enlisted March 10; transferred to cavalry; captain; killed.

McKim, Robert B.; enlisted July 6, 1861; killed at Winchester May 25, 1862.

Macon, Lyttleton S.; enlisted June 27, 1861; corporal, sergeant; discharged.

Magruder, Davenport D.; enlisted March 1, 1862; paroled at Appomattox.

Magruder, Horatio E.; paroled at Appomattox.

*Marshall, John J.; paroled at Appomattox.

Marshall, Oscar M.; enlisted March 6, 1862.

Massie, John Livingstone; enlisted May 15, 1861; captain of artillery; killed.

*Mateer, Samuel L.; enlisted January 11, 1863; paroled at Appomattox.

Maury, Magruder; enlisted in fall of 1861; transferred to cavalry.

Maury, Thompson B.; enlisted in fall of 1861; detailed in Signal Service.

Meade, Francis A.; enlisted November, 1862; paroled at Appomattox.

Merrick, Alfred D.; enlisted December 30, 1861.

Minor, Charles; enlisted November 16, 1861; became lieutenant of engineers.

Minor, C. N. Berkeley; enlisted July 27, 1861; became lieutenant of engineers.

Minor, Launcelot; wounded at Cumberland Church.

*Moore, Edward A.; enlisted March 3, 1862; wounded at Sharpsburg and twice at second Cold Harbor; paroled at Appomattox.

*Moore, John H.; transferred from Rockbridge Rifles in spring of 1861; wounded; paroled at Appomattox.

*Moore, John L.; enlisted July 23, 1861; wounded.

*Mooterspaugh, William; enlisted 1862; paroled at Appomattox.

Montgomery, Ben T.; transferred from another battery; paroled at Appomattox.

*Myers, John M.; paroled at Appomattox.

Nelson, Francis K.; enlisted May 17, 1861; transferred to Albemarle Light Horse.

Nelson, Kinloch; transferred from Albemarle Light Horse; disabled by caisson turning over on him; lieutenant Ordnance Department.

Nelson, Philip; enlisted July 27, 1861; discharged by furnishing substitute.

*Nicely, George H.; enlisted March 7, 1862; died from disease, 1864.

*Nicely, James W.; enlisted March 7, 1862; deserted.

*Nicely, John F.; enlisted July 23, 1861; wounded at Port Republic.

Otey, William M.; enlisted 1862; transferred soon thereafter.

Packard, Joseph; enlisted July 7, 1861; corporal; lientenant Ordnance Department.

Packard, Walter J.; enlisted October 23, 1861; died summer of 1862.

Page, Richard C. M.; enlisted July 14, 1861; transferred; captain; major artillery.

Page, R. Powell; enlisted May 1, 1864; detailed courier to Colonel Carter.

Paine, Henry M.

*Paine, Henry R.; enlisted July 23, 1861; corporal, sergeant; killed at second Manassas.

Paine, James A.

*Paxton, Samuel A.; enlisted March 7, 1862.

Pendleton, Dudley D.; enlisted June 19, 1861; captain and assistant adjutant-general, artillery A.N.V.

*Pleasants, Robert A.; enlisted March 3, 1863.

Pollard, James G.; enlisted July 27, 1864; paroled at Appomattox.

Porter, Mouina G.; enlisted September 24, 1861; detailed courier.

*Phillips, Charles; detailed in Signal Service.

*Pugh, George W.; enlisted March 6, 1862; paroled at Appomattox.

*Pugh, John A.; paroled at Appomattox.

Rawlings, James M.

*Rentzell, George W.; enlisted July 23, 1861; wounded at Kernstown and disabled.

*Robertson, John W.; paroled at Appomattox.

Robinson, Arthur; enlisted March 28, 1862; mortally wounded at first Fredericksburg.

*Root, Erastus C.; paroled at Appomattox.

Ruffin, Jefferson; transferred from another battery; paroled at Appomattox.

Rutledge, Charles A.; enlisted November 3, 1861; transferred.

*Sandford, James; paroled at Appomattox.

*Saville, John; enlisted July 23, 1861; transferred to cavalry; died in service.

*Shaner, Joseph F.; enlisted July 23, 1861; wounded at first Fredericksburg; paroled at Appomattox.

*Shaw, Campbell A.; paroled at Appomattox.

*Shoulder, Jacob M.; paroled at Appomattox.

Singleton, William F.; enlisted June 3, 1861; wounded and captured at Port Republic.

*Schammerhorn, John G.

Smith, J. Howard; enlisted September 2, 1861; lieutenant in Ordnance Department.

Smith, James P.; enlisted July 9, 1861; lieutenant and captain on staff of General Jackson.

Smith, James Morrison.

Smith, Summerfield; enlisted September 2, 1861; died from disease.

Stuart, G. W. C.; enlisted May 13, 1862; wounded
May 25, 1862; killed at second Fredericksburg.
*Strickler, Joseph; paroled at Appomattox.
*Stuart, W. C.; wounded at second Cold Harbor;
paroled at Appomattox.
Swan, Minor W.; enlisted August 15, 1863; paroled
at Appomattox.
Swan, Robert W.
*Swisher, Benjamin R.; enlisted March 3, 1862;
paroled at Appomattox.
*Swisher, George W.; enlisted March 3, 1862;
wounded May 25, 1862; paroled at Appomattox.
*Swisher, Samuel S.; paroled at Appomattox.
Tate, James F.; paroled at Appomattox.
Taylor, Charles F.
Taylor, Stevens M.; paroled at Appomattox.
Thompson, Ambrose; died July, 1864.
*Thompson, Lucas P.; enlisted August 15, 1861;
paroled at Appomattox.
Tidball, Thomas H.; enlisted March 3, 1862; pa-
roled at Appomattox.
*Timberlake, Francis H.
*Tomlinson, James W.; enlisted July 23, 1861.
Trice, Leroy F.; paroled at Appomattox.
Trueheart, Charles W.; enlisted October 24, 1861;
corporal, assistant surgeon.
Tyler, D. Gardner; paroled at Appomattox.
Tyler, John Alexander; enlisted April, 1865; pa-
roled at Appomattox.
*Van Pelt, Robert; enlisted July 23, 1861.

Veers, Charles O.; enlisted September 10, 1861; transferred to cavalry soon thereafter.

*Vest, Andrew J.; enlisted July 23, 1861; discharged.

*Wade, Thomas M.; enlisted March 7, 1862; paroled at Appomattox.

*Walker, George A.; enlisted July 23, 1861; transferred to Carpenter's battery.

*Walker, James S.; enlisted July 23, 1861; transferred to Carpenter's battery.

*Walker, John W.; enlisted July 23, 1861; transferred to Carpenter's battery.

Whitt, Algernon S.; enlisted August 8, 1861; corporal; paroled at Appomattox.

*White, William H.; paroled at Appomattox.

Williams, John J.; enlisted July 15, 1861; transferred to Chew's battery.

*Williamson, Thomas; wounded at Gettysburg; escaped at Appomattox with the cavalry.

*Williamson, William G.; enlisted July 5, 1861; captain of engineers.

*Wilson, Calvin.

*Wilson, John; enlisted July 22, 1861; prisoner after Gettysburg; took the oath.

*Wiseman, William; enlisted March 10, 1862.

*Wilson, Samuel A.; enlisted March 3, 1862; wounded at Gettysburg; captured; died in prison.

*Wilson, William M.; enlisted August 12, 1861; corporal.

Winston, Robert B.; enlisted August 25, 1861.

*Withrow, John; paroled at Appomattox.

*Woody, Henry; transferred from infantry, 1864; deserted.

*Wright, John W.; enlisted 1864; wounded and disabled at Spottsylvania Court House.

Young, Charles E.; enlisted March 17, 1862.

The Rockbridge Artillery took part in the following engagaments:

Hainesville, July 2, 1861.

First Manassas, July 21, 1861.

Kernstown, March 23, 1862.

Winchester, May 25, 1862.

Charlestown, May, 1862.

Port Republic, June 8 and 9, 1862.

White Oak Swamp, June 30, and Malvern Hill, July 1, 1862.

Cedar Run, August 9, 1862.

Second Manassas, August 28, 29 and 30, 1862.

Harper's Ferry, September 15, 1862.

Sharpsburg, September 17, 1862.

First Fredericksburg, December 13, 1862.

Second Fredericksburg, May 2 and 3, 1863.

Winchester, June 14, 1863.

Gettysburg, July 2 and 3, 1863.

Rappahannock Bridge, November 9, 1863.

Mine Run, November 27, 1863.

Spottsylvania Court House, May 12, 1864.

Cold Harbor, June 3, 1864.

Deep Bottom, July 27, 1864.

New Market Heights, September, 1864.
Fort Gilmore, 1864.
Cumberland Church, April 7, 1865.

The battery saw much service in fighting gunboats on James River, and took part in many skirmishes not mentioned.

The number of men, enrolled as above, is three hundred and five (305), of whom one hundred and seventy-three (173) were from the county of Rockbridge. Of the remainder, a large part were students, college graduates, University of Virginia men, and some divinity students. These, with the sturdy men from among the farmers and business men of Rockbridge, made up a company admirably fitted for the artillery service.

The efficiency of the battery was due in no small part to its capacity for rapid marching and maneuvering, and this to the care and management of the horses mainly by men from this county. In the spring of 1862 a large number of men was recruited for the battery, whose names are not on the above roll, and some of whom were engaged in the battle of Kernstown. In April, 1862, while encamped at Swift Run Gap, authority was given by General Jackson to reorganize the battery, making three companies thereof, with the view to form a battalion. Immediately after two companies had been organized by the election of officers, the authority for making three companies was revoked, and an order issued to form one company only, and giving to all the men not embraced in this one company the privilege of selecting a company in any branch of the service. A large number of men, thus temporarily connected with the Rockbridge Artillery, availed themselves of this privilege whose names do not appear on the above roll. It would now be impossible to make up this list.

RECAPITULATION

Enrolled as above, three hundred and five (305).

Number from Rockbridge County, one hundred and seventy-three (173).

Killed in battle, twenty-three (23).

Died of disease contracted in service, sixteen (16).

Wounded more or less severely, forty-nine (49).

Slightly wounded, names not given, about fifty (50).

Discharged from service for disability incurred therein, ten (10).

Took the oath of allegiance to Federal Government while in prison, two (2).

Deserted, five (5).

Promoted to be commissioned officers, thirty-nine (39).

Paroled at Appomattox, ninety-three (93).

So great was the loss of horses, there having been over a hundred in this battery killed in battle, that during the last year of the war they were unhitched from the guns after going into action and taken to the rear for safety.